◎ 普通高校专业英语教程系列

会计专业
英语教程

宋德富　瞿天易　苑庆春　主编

清华大学出版社
北京

内 容 简 介

本书涵盖两大板块内容。第一板块围绕会计等式讲解会计基本要素，包括资产、债务、权益、资产负债表、收付实现制和权责发生制等；第二板块围绕常用的会计业务展开，包括复式记账、日记账分录、保本点分析、公认的会计准则、国际财务报告准则等。本书涉及广泛的会计专业内容，基础会计英语术语总结全面，适合作为会计专业本科和硕士的学习材料，也可作为会计相关从业人员的自学材料。

图书在版编目（CIP）数据

会计专业英语教程 / 宋德富，瞿天易，苑庆春主编. —北京：清华大学出版社，2023.10
普通高校专业英语教程系列
ISBN 978-7-302-54314-5

Ⅰ.①会…　Ⅱ.①宋…②瞿…③苑…　Ⅲ.①会计学—英语—高等学校—教材　Ⅳ.① F230

中国版本图书馆 CIP 数据核字（2019）第 262843 号

责任编辑：徐博文
封面设计：何凤霞
责任校对：王凤芝
责任印制：刘海龙

出版发行：清华大学出版社
　　　　　网　　　址：https://www.tup.com.cn, https://www.wqxuetang.com
　　　　　地　　　址：北京清华大学学研大厦 A 座　　　　邮　　编：100084
　　　　　社 总 机：010-83470000　　　　　　　　　　邮　　购：010-62786544
　　　　　投稿与读者服务：010-62776969, c-service@tup.tsinghua.edu.cn
　　　　　质量反馈：010-62772015, zhiliang@tup.tsinghua.edu.cn
印 装 者：大厂回族自治县彩虹印刷有限公司
经　　销：全国新华书店
开　　本：185mm×260mm　　　　印　　张：7　　　　字　　数：150 千字
版　　次：2023 年 12 月第 1 版　　　　　　　　印　　次：2023 年 12 月第 1 次印刷
定　　价：58.00 元

产品编号：081234-01

前　言

在本教程编辑的时候，中国的改革开放已经走过了四十多个年头，其间，中国的会计制度正逐步与世界接轨。中华人民共和国财政部在 1992 年 1 月针对股份合作制公司颁布了一个单独的会计管理条例《企业会计标准》，开启了向国际会计标准趋同的征程。中国第一个公司法到 1994 年 7 月才生效。1999 年的《中华人民共和国会计法》和 2001 年的《企业财务会计报告条例》的颁布，使不同企业的不同会计标准和条例得到了协调，中国现代会计框架自此才算清晰了起来。2007 年 1 月开始实施的《企业会计准则》与国际财务报告准则（IFRS）的基本趋向一致，只是在措辞方面有一些细微的差异。

为了更好地服务中国经济的发展，支持中国企业"走出去"，中国注册会计师行业积极推进行业的国际化进程，制定了行业人才培养战略、准则国际趋同战略和事务所"做大做强"战略。其中，培养具有国际化资质、获得国际资本市场认可的行业人才队伍是行业人才培养战略的重要内容，也是实现会计师事务所"做大做强"和"走出去"的基础条件。为此，中国注册会计师协会（中注协 CICPA）与境外知名会计师职业组织合作，加快中国注册会计师行业国际化人才的培养进程。

人才的培养在学校，这就迫切要求我国高校必须为培养熟练操作国际财务报告准则的毕业生打下良好的基础，以满足社会经济发展的需求。会计专业英语是国际会计专业学生不可或缺的学习课程。但该课程在高校会计专业中的开设比率并不高，原因是缺少会计专业英语教师、学生基础英语不扎实、没有合适的、高质量的会计英语教材等。随着高等教育的进步，一方面，高校会计教师队伍中出现了为数不少的、有英语国家会计专业学习背景的学者，这为会计英语课程的开设准备了教师队伍；另一方面，大学英语四、六级通过率逐年提升，学生为学习专业英语夯实了基础。

本教程适合作为会计专业英语的必修课教材。本教程的教学重点在于解析课文 A 的长难句，提升学生阅读会计英语材料的能力，为未来参加各种会计英语考试和从业做好准备。本教程注重归纳会计专业英语术语，为学生的阅读、口语表述和会计英语写作夯实基础。教师要鼓励学生通过查找网络资源独立完成教程中的大量练习，培养他们的自学能力。本教程配有丰富的教学资源，包括练习参考答案、课文 B 的译文以及形式丰富的电子课件，读者可到清华大学出版社官方网站下载。

本教程的编者具有丰富的会计专业英语教材编写经验，接受清华大学出版社的邀约编写了这本会计专业英语教程，冀望得到广大用户的厚爱。编者在编写时遇到的难题得到了

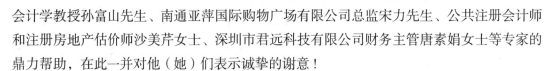

会计学教授孙富山先生、南通亚萍国际购物广场有限公司总监宋力先生、公共注册会计师和注册房地产估价师沙美芹女士、深圳市君远科技有限公司财务主管唐素娟女士等专家的鼎力帮助，在此一并对他（她）们表示诚挚的谢意！

由于经济形势发展千变万化，会计行业规则也在不断地发展变化，囿于编者水平和阅历，本教程难免存在不尽如人意的地方，敬请教学一线的老师和会计界的专家达人不吝赐教，以便修订新版时吸纳改进，确保本教程与时俱进，充满活力，永葆青春。

编　者

2023 年 8 月

Contents

Unit 1

Unit 2

Unit 3

Unit 4

Unit 5

Unit 6

Unit 7

Unit 8

Unit 9

Unit 10

Unit

1

Accounting for Business

Introduction

[1] A strong company can attribute some of its success to its accounting. Without accounting, it would be hard to keep track of your business's finances and profitability, and you might not know exactly how much money is coming in or going out.

[2] Unless you are well-versed in finance yourself, your business will likely need to enlist the help of a professional accountant. Here's a breakdown of who accountants are and what they do for your company.

What do accountants do?

[3] The American Accounting Association defines accounting as "the process of identifying, measuring and communicating economic information to permit informed judgments and decisions by users of the information". Logging a business's account payable, accounts receivable and other financial transactions, typically using accounting software, is often how it's done.

[4] "Accountants use the work done by bookkeepers to produce and analyze financial reports," said Stan Snyder. "Although accounting follows the same principles and rules as bookkeeping, an accountant can design a system that will capture all of the details necessary to satisfy the needs of the business—managerial, financial reporting, projection, analysis and tax reporting."

[5] In the United States, most accountants abide by the Generally Accepted Accounting Principles to present a company's financial information to those outside of the company in a format that everyone can understand. There are different sets of accounting standards for companies that operate overseas, as well as for local and state government entities.

[6] Harold Averkamp, CPA and owner of Accounting Coach, said accountants also provide a company's internal management team with the information it needs to keep the business financially healthy. Some of the information will originate from the recorded transactions, while some will consist of estimates and projections based on various assumptions, he said.

Accounting ratios

[7] Accounting ratios help uncover conditions and trends that are difficult to find by inspecting individual components that make up the ratio, and formulas like this help accountants to come up with a company's status and projections. Accounting ratios are divided into five main categories:

- Liquidity ratios: measure liquid assets of the company versus its liabilities.
- Profitability ratios: measure organization's ability to turn a profit after paying expenses.
- Leverage ratios: measure total debt versus total assets and gauge equity.
- Turnover ratios: measure efficiency by comparing cost of goods sold over a period of time against amount of inventory that was on hand during that same time.
- Market-value ratios: measure company's economic status compared with others in industry.

Accounting careers

[8] Many accountants within the industry choose to become CPAs, achieved by passing an exam and getting work experience. The Pennsylvania Institute of Certified Public Accountants explains that CPAs audit financial statements of public and private companies, serve as consultants in many areas, including tax, accounting and financial planning, and are well-respected strategic business advisors and decision-makers. The role of a CPA ranges from accountants to controllers and from chief financial officers of Fortune 500 companies to advisors for small neighborhood businesses.

Basic accounting tasks

[9] • Record transactions. Depending on volume, an accountant will record each transaction (billing customers, receiving cash from customers, paying vendors, etc.) daily or weekly.

- Document and file receipts. Copy all invoices sent, all cash receipts (cash, check and credit card deposits) and all cash payments (cash, check, credit card statements, etc.), and start a filing system that makes sense, easy to keep track of, and easy to maintain.
- Pay vendors, sign checks. Track your accounts payable and have funds scheduled to pay your suppliers on time to avoid late fees.
- Balance your business checkbook. This task is done monthly to insure that your cash business transaction entries are accurate and that you are working with the correct cash position.

- Process or review payroll and approve tax payments. You need to meet payroll tax requirements based on federal, state and local laws at different times, so be sure to withhold, report and deposit the applicable income tax, social security, medicare and disability taxes to the appropriate agencies on the required dates.

New Words

abide [ə'baid] *vt. & vi.* 遵守

applicable [ə'plikəbl] *adj.* 合适的

audit ['ɔ:dit] *vt. & vi.* 审计，查账　*n.* 审计，查账

bill [bil] *n.* 账单；钞票；清单　*vt.* 给……开账单；为……发提（货）单

bookkeeping ['bʊkki:piŋ] *n.* 记账，簿记，管账

breakdown ['breikdaʊn] *n.* 分解

checkbook ['tʃekˌbʊk] *n.* 支票本（=cheque-book）；账本；账户

consultant [kən'sʌltənt] *n.* （受人咨询的）顾问

enlist [in'list] *vt.* 赢得……的支持或合作

entity ['entəti] *n.* 实体；机关

equity ['ekwəti] *n.* 权益，资产净值；股票

format ['fɔ:mæt] *n.* 格式

formula ['fɔ:mjələ] *n.* 公式，准则；方案，方式

gauge [geidʒ] *n.* 标准，规范

identify [ai'dentifai] *vt. & vi.* 识别，认出，确定

informed [in'fɔ:md] *adj.* 有情报根据的；信息充分的

inventory ['invəntri] *n.* 存货总值；存货清单

invoice ['invɔis] *n.* 发票；发货单　*vt.* 为……开发票；记清单

liability [ˌlaiə'biləti] *n.* 债务

log [lɔg] *vt.* 把……载入正式记录

payable ['peiəbl] *adj.* 应付的，可付的　*n.* 应付款，应付项

payroll ['peirəʊl] *n.* 工资名单；工资总额

professional [prə'feʃənl] *adj.* 专业的，专业性的，职业的　*n.* 专业人士

profitability [prɔfitə'biləti] *n.* 获利（状况），盈利（情况）

projection [prə'dʒekʃən] *n.* 预测，规划，设计

receipt [ri'si:t] *n.* 收据，发票；收入　*vt.* 为……开收据

receivable [ri'si:vəbl] *adj.* 可收到的　*n.*（常*pl.*）应收账款

turnover ['tə:nəʊvə(r)] *n.* 周转；营业额，成交量

vendor ['vendə(r)] *n.* 小贩，小供应商

versed [və:st] *adj.* 精通的，熟练的

versus ['və:səs] *prep.* 与……相对，与……相比

withhold [wið'həʊld] *vt.* 扣留；扣交

Special Terms

accounting ratio 会计率	government entity 政府机关
accounting standard 会计标准，会计准则	late fee 滞纳金
American Accounting Association 美国会计协会	leverage ratio 杠杆率
	liquid asset 流动资产
cash receipt 现金收入	liquidity ratio 流动比率
credit card deposit (statement) 信用卡存款（对账单）	market-value ratio 市值率
	profitability ratio 利润率
document/file receipt 收款单据	sign check 符号校验
filing system 档案系统	social security 社会保险
financial transaction 财务往来	turnover ratio 周转率
financial statement 财务报告	withholding tax 预扣税
gauge equity 规范股权	

 **Abbreviations**

CPA (Certified Public Accountant) 注册会计师
GAAP (Generally Accepted Accounting Principles) 普遍接受的会计原则 / 准则 / 标准，公认会计准则

 Notes

Paras. [1] to [2]

1. A strong company can attribute some of its success to its accounting.
   "attribute success to..." 的意思是 "把成功归功于……"。全句可译为：一个强大的公司可以把它的某些成果归功于会计工作。

2. ... enlist the help of a professional accountant...：寻求职业会计的帮助

Para. [3]

3. ... defines accounting as the process of identifying, measuring and communicating economic information to permit informed judgments and decisions by users of the information.

"economic information" 前面有三个动名词：identifying、measuring and communicating，意思为"鉴别、测评和交流（经济信息）"；"informed judgments and decisions"指"根据信息进行的判断和形成的决议"。这句话说的是美国会计协会对会计的定义，即对经济信息进行鉴别、测评和交流，从而使信息用户能够做出有据的判定并形成正确的决策的过程。

4. Logging a business's account payable, accounts receivable and other financial transactions, typically using accounting software, is often how it's done.

这句的主语是 logging，逻辑宾语是 a business's account payable, accounts receivable and other financial transactions；payable 和 receivable 是两个后置形容词，形容记录企业的收支账户；typically using accounting software 是插入语，表示这种记录通常使用会计软件完成；在由 how 引导的表语从句中，it 指 accounting（会计工作）。全句可译为：通常，会计工作就是使用会计软件记录公司的收支账户和其他的财务事项。

Paras. [7] to [9]

5. Accounting ratios help uncover conditions and trends that are difficult to find by inspecting individual components that make up the ratio, and formulas like this help accountants to come up with a company's status and projections.

这个长句包含两个并列分句。第一个分句的主语是 Accounting ratios；help uncover conditions and trends，即"帮助揭示状况和趋势"，其后为一个由 that 引导的定语从句，说明这种状况和趋势不是通过观察形成比率的个别因素能够发现的。第二个分句的主语是 formulas like this。全句可译为：会计比率有助于揭示公司的现状和发展趋势，但如果只是观察构成这些比率的个别因素，是很难发现的，而这些比率的计算公式能够帮助会计人员报告公司的状况以及提出未来的规划。

6. The Pennsylvania Institute of Certified Public Accountants explains that CPAs audit financial statements of public and private companies; serve as consultants in many areas, including tax, accounting and financial planning; and are well-respected strategic business advisors and decision-makers.

本句主语是 The Pennsylvania Institute of Certified Public Accountants（宾夕法尼亚注册会计师协会），谓语动词 explain 后有一个 that 从句，从句主语是 CPAs，它有三个谓语动词：audit、serve as、are。全句可译为：宾夕法尼亚注册会计师协会解释道：注册会计师审计公共和私人公司财务报表。他们在很多部门，包括税务、会计和财务规划部门担任咨询工作，是非常受人尊重的公司战略顾问和决策人员。

7. ... start a filing system that makes sense, easy to keep track of, and easy to maintain.

本句描述的是会计工作开启的档案系统。本句的 that 定语分句后有三个并列谓语：makes sense（具有实际意义）、easy to keep track of（易于跟踪）、easy to maintain（易于保持）。

8. ... be sure to withhold, report and deposit the applicable income tax, social security, medicare and disability taxes to the appropriate agencies on the required dates.

本句的 be sure 后有三个不定式动词：(to) withhold（代扣）、(to) report（报告）、(to) deposit

（存款），它们的宾语分别是 the applicable income tax（合适的所得税）、social security（社保）、medicare and disability taxes（医疗和残疾人税）。全句可译为：要完成代扣、报税和把款项存入规定账号向规定机构，在规定的日期内缴纳社保、医疗和残疾人税收。

Exercises

Ex. 1 **Decide whether the following statements are true (T) or false (F) according to the information in Passage A.**

(1) The company has become very strong, whose accounting is sure to be successful. (   )

(2) In order to master your business finances and profitability, you should manage the finance yourself. (   )

(3) Typically a boss can be well-versed in finance so he or she doesn't need a professional accountant. (   )

(4) Accountants provide correct economic information only for inside users. (   )

(5) Correct economic information ensures users to form correct judgments and make right decisions. (   )

(6) High leverage ratio means that the business bears the burden of an enormous debt. (   )

(7) High market-value ratio means the company is competitive in the market. (   )

(8) By passing an exam, one can become a CPA. (   )

(9) A CPA is qualified as an auditor. (   )

(10) An accountant must record each transaction daily. (   )

Ex. 2 **Match each of the words in the box to each of the following eight phrases or definitions that is most closely related.**

A. versed	B. profitability	C. liability	D. projection
E. receipt	F. formula	G. inventory	H. invoice

(1) an estimate of a future amount (   )

(2) skilled in, thoroughly knowledgeable about (   )

(3) a writing acknowledging the receiving of goods or money (   )

(4) a company's financial debt or obligations that arise during the course of its business operations (   )

(5) the collection of unsold products waiting to be sold (   )

(6) the ability to make a profit (   )

(7) a commercial document issued by a seller to a buyer (   )

(8) a mathematical rule expressed in a set of numbers and letters (   )

Ex. 3 Use the terms or vocabularies mentioned in Ex. 2 to complete the following sentences. Change the form if necessary.

(1) By 2075, the United Nations' mid-range _____ for global population is about 9.5 billion.

(2) The _____ of calculating the leverage ratio is total debt versus total assets and gauge equity.

(3) A clerk simply verifies that the payment and _____ mount match.

(4) After I paid the money, the shop assistant gave me a (n) _____.

(5) These experts are more _____ in the economics of taxes than the politics of taxes.

(6) _____ is listed as a current asset on a company's balance sheet.

(7) A joint venture is a limited _____.

(8) Safety, liquidity, _____ of commercial banks has always been a goal.

Ex. 4 Fill in the blanks with the words or phrases given in the box. Change the form if necessary.

attribute	log	uncover	come up with
withhold	keep track of	enlist	abide

(1) Everyone should _____ by our social norms.

(2) Police _____ the kidnapper using electronic surveillance equipment.

(3) Several of the members _____ suggestions of their own.

(4) The password allows the user _____ into the system.

(5) We ought to look below the surface of things and then _____ the essence of them.

(6) The fall in the number of deaths from heart disease _____ generally improvements in diet.

(7) Money that is taken out of your wages as tax is _____ tax.

(8) The conference will make further efforts _____ the support of the international community for their just struggle.

Ex. 5 Complete the following short passage with the words and phrases given in the box.

A. financial accounting	B. projections
C. Generally Accepted Accounting Principles	D. assumptions
E. management accounting	F. computer technology
G. transactions	H. income tax

One part of accounting focuses on presenting the information in the form of general-purpose financial statements (balance sheet, income statement, etc.) to people outside of the company. These external reports must be prepared in accordance with (1) _____ often referred to as GAAP or US GAAP. This part of accounting is referred to as (2) _____.

Accounting also entails providing a company's management with the information it needs to keep the business financially healthy. These analyses and reports are not distributed outside of the company. Some of the information will originate from the recorded (3) _____ but some of the information will be estimates and (4) _____ based on various (5) _____. Three examples of internal analyses and reports are budgets, standards for controlling operations, and estimating selling prices for quoting new jobs. This area of accounting is known as (6)_____. Another part of accounting involves compliance with government regulations pertaining to (7) _____ reporting. Today much of the recording, storing, and sorting aspects of accounting have been automated as a result of the advances in (8) _____.

Passage B

A Story for Relating to Accounting Basics

[1] We will present the basics of accounting through a story of a person starting a new business. The person is Joe Perez—a savvy man who sees the need for a parcel delivery service in his community. Joe has researched his idea and has prepared a business plan that documents the viability of his new business.

[2] Joe has also met with an attorney to discuss the form of business he should use. Given his specific situation, they concluded that a corporation will be best. Joe decides that the name for his corporation will be Direct Delivery, Inc. The attorney also advises Joe on the various permits and government identification numbers that will be needed for the new corporation.

[3] Joe is a hard worker and a smart man, but he is not comfortable with matters of accounting. He assumes he will use some accounting software, but wants to meet with a professional accountant before making his selection. He asks his banker to recommend a professional accountant who is also skilled in explaining accounting to someone without an accounting background. Joe wants to understand the financial statements and wants to keep on top of his new business. His banker recommends Marilyn, an accountant who has helped many of the bank's small business customers.

[4] At his first meeting with Marilyn, Joe asks her for an overview of accounting, financial statements, and the need for accounting software. Based on Joe's business plan, Marilyn sees that there will likely be thousands of transactions each year. She states that accounting software will allow for the electronic recording, storing, and retrieval of those many transactions. Accounting software will permit Joe to generate the financial statements and other reports that he will need for running his business.

[5] Joe seems puzzled by the term transaction, so Marilyn gives him five examples of transactions that Direct Delivery, Inc. will need to record:

(1) Joe will no doubt start his business by putting some of his own personal money into it. In effect, he is buying shares of Direct Delivery's common stock.

(2) Direct Delivery will need to buy a sturdy, dependable delivery vehicle.

(3) The business will begin earning fees and billing clients for delivering their parcels.

(4) The business will be collecting the fees that were earned.

(5) The business will incur expenses in operating the business, such as a salary for Joe, expenses associated with the delivery vehicle, advertising, etc.

[6] With thousands of such transactions in a given year, Joe is smart to start using accounting software right from the beginning. Accounting software will generate sales invoices and accounting entries simultaneously, prepare statements for customers with no additional work, write checks, automatically update accounting records, etc.

[7] By getting into the habit of entering all of the day's business transactions into his computer, Joe will be rewarded with fast and easy access to the specific information he will need to make sound business decisions. Marilyn tells Joe that accounting's "transaction approach" is useful, reliable, and informative. She has worked with other small business owners who think it is enough to simply "know" their company made $30,000 during the year (based only on the fact that it owns $30,000 more than it did on January 1. Those are the people who start off on the wrong foot and end up in Marilyn's office looking for financial advice.

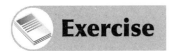

Exercise

Decide whether the following statements are true (T) or false (F) according to the information in Passage B.

(1) A business plan is a necessary document to create a new business. (   )

(2) Direct Delivery is the name of the corporation Joe Perez is going to join. (   )

(3) A new corporation needs various permits and government identification numbers. (   )

(4) Joe is well-versed in the accounting. (   )

(5) Marilyn is a professional accountant the banker has recommended to Joe. (   )

(6) Marilyn holds the view that accounting software is necessary for Joe's new corporation. (   )

(7) Marilyn tells Joe he should record all his transactions by using the accounting software. (   )

(8) "Billing clients" means presenting bills to customers. (   )

(9) Salary for Joe himself doesn't need to be recorded. (   )

(10) Accounting software can issue sales invoices. (   )

Unit

2

How to Use the Accounting Equation

[1] As a small business owner, it's important to understand information about your company's finances. One important thing to look at is how much of your business assets are financed with debt vs. paid for with capital. Use the accounting equation to see the differences.

What is the accounting equation

[2] The accounting equation is used in double-entry accounting. It shows the relationship between your business's assets, liabilities, and equity. By using the accounting equation, you can see if your assets are financed by debt or business funds. The accounting equation is also called the balance sheet equation.

Balance sheet equation parts

[3] Use your business's balance sheet to calculate the accounting equation. The balance sheet is a financial statement that tracks your company's progress. The balance sheet has three parts: assets, liabilities, and equity.

[4] Assets are items of value that your business owns. For example, your business bank account, company vehicles, and equipment are assets.

[5] Liabilities are debts that you owe to others. For example, your payables are liabilities.

[6] Business equity shows your ownership in the business. If you are a sole proprietor, you hold all the ownership. If there is more than one owner, you split the equity. Calculate equity by subtracting your assets from liabilities.

What is the basic accounting equation

[7] The accounting equation requires liabilities and equity to equal assets. The following is the accounting calculation: Assets = Liabilities + Equity.

[8] Each side of the accounting equation has to equal the other because you must purchase things with either debt or capital.

[9] Equity has an equal effect on both sides of the equation. If you know any two parts of the accounting equation, you can calculate the third. You can write the accounting equation with the liabilities by itself: Liabilities = Assets – Equity. Or, you can write the accounting equation with equity by itself: Equity = Assets – Liabilities.

Accounting equation examples

[10] The following examples are connected to the same business. Take a look at how different ownership affects the accounting equation. Then, see the business's balance sheet at the end of this section.

[11] Example 1: You're starting a business selling printed T-shirts. You save for a year before opening and contribute $10,000 to the new company. By doing this, you increase your business's assets and owner's equity by the same amount: Assets ($10,000) = Liabilities + Equity ($10,000).

[12] Example 2: Let's say that after you form your company, you need to buy equipment to print the T-shirts. You purchase $2,000 of the equipment on credit. In this situation, you gain a liability (debt) and an asset. Your assets and liabilities increase by $2,000, so the equation looks like: Assets ($2,000) = Liabilities ($2,000) + Equity.

[13] Example 3: As your T-shirt company grows, you get an order for 50 shirts from a customer. The customer pays $10 per shirt, or $500 total. You gain an asset and equity from the transaction: Assets ($500) = Liabilities + Equity ($500).

Example balance sheet

[14] You will record each of the above transactions on the balance sheet. The assets should equal the liabilities plus equity. Here is the full accounting equation for this example: Assets ($12,500) = Liabilities ($2,000) + Equity ($10,500).

Expanded accounting equation

[15] The expanded accounting equation shows the relationship between your income statement and balance sheet. You can see how equity is created from its two main sources: revenue and owner contributions. This expanded the accounting equation: Assets = Liabilities + Owner's Equity + Revenue – Expenses – Draws

[16] Revenues are what your business earns through regular operations. Expenses are what it costs to provide your products and services. Certain patterns occur as figures in the expanded accounting equation change:

Revenue increases owner's equity;

Expenses decrease owner's equity;

Owner's draw decreases owner's equity.

[17] The two sides of the equation must equal each other. If the expanded accounting equation is not balanced, your financial reports are inaccurate.

Why is the accounting equation important?

[18] The accounting equation can give you a clear picture of your business's financial situation. You must calculate the accounting equation to read your balance sheet. The accounting equation helps you understand the relationship between your financial statements. In an article, Heather D. Satterley, founder of Satterley Training & Consulting, LLC, explains:

[19] The purpose of the balance sheet is to show the financial position of the business on any given day. The balance sheet can tell you how much money the business has in the bank and how likely it is that the business will be able to meet all of its financial obligations. It can also tell you how much profit (or loss) the business has retained since it started.

[20] By using the accounting equation, you can see if you can fund the purchase of an asset with your business's existing assets. And, the equation will reveal if you should pay off debts with assets (like cash) or by taking on more liabilities.

 **New Words**

equation [i'kweiʃən] *n.* 方程式，等式；相等	sole [səul] *adj.* 单独的，唯一的；专有的
double-entry ['dʌbl-'entri] *n.* 复式记账	credit ['kredit] *n.* 贷记；信誉，信用；贷款；学分 *vt.* 记入贷方
proprietor [prə'praiətə] *n.* 所有人，业主	contribution [kəntri'bju:ʃn] *n.* 投入，投资
subtract [səb'trækt] *vt.* 减去，扣除	inaccurate [in'ækjərət] *adj.* 有错误的，不精密的；不正确的

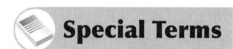 **Special Terms**

accounting equation 会计方程式	on credit 赊账
double-entry accounting 复式会计	income statement 收入报表
balance sheet 资产负债表	financial obligation 财务义务
business equity 企业权益，企业股本	business fund 企业基金，业务基金
sole proprietor 独资经营者；独资企业	balance sheet equation 资产负债方程式

 **Abbreviations**

vs. (versus)（表示两队或双方对阵）对；（比较两种不同想法、选择等）与……相对

LLC (Limited Liability Company) 有限（责任）公司

Notes

Para. [1]

1. One important thing to look at is how much of your business assets are financed with debt vs. paid for with capital.

本句中的 financed with debt 意思是"依靠债务提供资金；paid for with capital 意思是"用资本（本金）支付"。本句提示了一件小企业需要关心的事，那就是看看自己的企业有多少资产是依赖债务提供的资金，又有多少资产是通过自身的资本支付的。

Para. [7]

2. The accounting equation requires liabilities and equity to equal assets.

本句可译为：会计公式要求债务和股本之和等于资产。

Paras. [18] to [19]

3. Heather D. Satterley: the founder of Satterley Training & Consulting, LLC.

赫特·D. 萨特里创建了为有限责任公司创业者服务的萨特里培训咨询网站。

4. ... how likely it is that the business will be able to meet all of its financial obligations.

本句中的 likely 为形容词，表示"可能的"，用于句型 It is likely that... 表示可能性。... how likely it is that... 即"会有……的可能性"。全句描述的是企业履行财务债务的能力可能的状态。

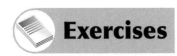 **Exercises**

Ex. 1 **Decide whether the following statements are true (T) or false (F) according to the information in Passage A.**

(1) A small business has to pay for its assets with business fund. (　　)

(2) A small business can also finance its assets with liabilities. (　　)

(3) A finance statement is not the balance sheet. (　　)

(4) Assets do not include the liabilities. (　　)

(5) The leverage ratio of a business is that liabilities are divided by assets. (　　)

(6) To increase the business's assets means to increase owner's equity. (　　)

(7) Liabilities add to owner's equity. (　　)

(8) Assets' change is sure to lead to that of both liabilities and equities. (　　)

(9) Owner contributions do not belong to owner's equity. (　　)

(10) Taking on more liabilities can add to the assets of your company. (　　)

Ex. 2 **Match each of the words in the box to the following phrases or definitions that is most closely related.**

A. capital	B. asset	C. payable	D. ownership
E. credit	F. transaction	G. equity	H. revenue

(1) that may, can, or must be paid (　　)

(2) the state or fact of being an owner (　　)

(3) borrowed money that you can use to purchase goods and services when you need them (　　)

(4) assets and cash in a business (　　)

(5) exchange of goods or services between a buyer and a seller (　　)

(6) a possession of a business that will bring the business benefits in the future (　　)

(7) the income generated from sale of goods or services, or any other use of capital or assets, associated with the main operations of an organization before any costs or expenses are deducted (　　)

(8) funds contributed by the owners (stockholders) plus retained earnings or minus the accumulated losses (　　)

Ex. 3 **Use the words mentioned in Ex. 2 to complete the following sentences. Change the form if necessary.**

(1) An account _____ at one company is an account receivable for the vendor that issued the sales invoice.

(2) Buying a house is an important _____ for most people.

(3) Large companies have a difficult time switching into new markets because there is a temptation to put existing _____ into the new businesses.

(4) On a company's balance sheet, the amount of the funds contributed by the owners (the shareholders) plus the retained earnings (or losses) is owner's _____.

(5) In general usage, _____ is income received by an organization in the form of cash or cash equivalents.

(6) A business owner's account is sometimes called owner's equity or the owner's _____ account.

(7) The _____ of the company changed hands once the gentleman acquired 51% of the company and new policies were implemented.

(8) A (n) _____ grantor is the person or the bank you agree to pay back the amount you spent, plus applicable finance charges, at an agreed-upon time.

Ex. 4 **Fill in the blanks with the words and phrases given in the box. Change the form if necessary.**

retain	fund	pay off	take on
finance	track	owe	contribute

(1) The company _____ $618 million to its creditors.

(2) Modern airplanes have two black boxes: a voice recorder, which _____ pilots' conversations, and a flight-data recorder, which monitors fuel levels, engine noises and other operating functions that help investigators reconstruct the aircraft's final moments.

(3) Alternative forms of energy-bio-fuels, wind and solar, to name a few, are certainly being _____ and developed, and will play a growing role in the world's energy supply.

(4) The villagers _____ a strong attachment to their traditional customs.

(5) You might also _____ other assets, like a computer, some equipment, or a vehicle that will be owned by the business.

(6) In view of long commuting distances to work, the new car was often a relief which could only _____ by working overtime.

(7) Don't _____ more loads than you can meet.

(8) When their business failed, the family closed ranks and worked _____ the debts.

Ex. 5 **Read the following short passage and then complete the multiple choice.**

Satterley, Founder of Satterley Training & Consulting LLC

I know how to help you because I've been in your shoes. In my work traveling the country teaching QuickBooks Online, I have learned that many of you struggle with the same things I have: developing the processes to efficiently run and scale your practice.

My perspective is fueled by my experience working at firms of all sizes, from my one-person bookkeeping shop to an organization of nearly 100 people. Regardless of the size of the organization I worked in, I used technology to transform my workflow and processes. As I found solutions that made life easier for me and my clients, my business grew. My workflow made it easier to hire and train new employees. Now my passion is helping you.

My qualifications span nearly 20 years. As an Enrolled Agent, authorized to practice before the IRS (Internal Revenue Service), I have insight into how to provide tax clients with the service they desire. A ProAdvisor (pro means professional) since 1999, I am also part of the Intuit Trainer/Writer Network. I have co-authored the QuickBooks Online (QuickBooks is an accounting software package developed and marketed by Intuit.) and Desktop Advanced Certification training and exams. I have been named as a Top 100 ProAdvisor by *Insightful Accountant Online Magazine* in 2014, 2015, 2016 and 2017.

(1) "I've been in your shoes" means _____.

    A. I have bought a pair of shoes for you

    B. the size of my shoes is the same as that of yours

    C. I'm in the position just as you

    D. we're in the same boat

(2) "Scale your practice" means _____.

    A. your practice scope is larger and larger

    B. you are climbing in the process of running your business

    C. you are practicing running your business

    D. you've been successful in running your business

(3) "My perspective is fueled by my experience working at firms of all sizes…" Which of the four explanations is suitable for the word "perspective"?

    A. the appearance to the eye of objects in respect to their relative distance and positions

    B. a visible scene

    C. point of view

    D. a particular way of viewing things that depends on one's experience and personality

(4) Which of the following statements is FALSE?

    A. Satterley strictly abided by the workflow and processes whether she worked in a big or small organization.

    B. Satterley found solutions making life easier for her and her clients.

    C. Satterley is not working in an organization now.

    D. An enrolled agent is a person who has earned the privilege of representing tax payers.

(5) Which of the following statements is FALSE?

    A. Desktop Advanced Certification training and exams are the task of the Intuit Trainer/Writer Network.

    B. Satterley has finished the accounting software package QuickBooks alone.

    C. Top 100 ProAdvisor is published by *Insightful Accountant Online Magazine*.

    D. Top 100 ProAdvisor is published once a year.

Passage B

Basic Elements of Accounting

[1] The purpose of accounting is to present a precise financial picture of your business operations. By convention, financial accounting consists of five basic elements, and when you prepare financial records, each activity will touch at least one of these elements. The accounting convention further explains how to record these elements, whether as increases or decreases in debit and credit columns. Debit and credit entries in an accounting journal are simply entries made in the respective right and left columns. Each transaction requires a double entry, one to record the debit and the other to record the credit.

Assets

[2] Assets are the resources you use to conduct your business activities. To record an item as an asset, you must own it or have a right to control and use it. For example, if you own a delivery business, your delivery truck likely meets this requirement. Assets also must provide some future economic benefit to your business. Economic benefits can include cash and credit sales. Since you use your truck to deliver goods to your customers, your truck allows you to reap an economic benefit—sales—and meets this criterion as well. To record an increase in an asset, you debit the account, and a credit records a decrease.

Liabilities

[3] Liabilities are your company's current obligations. They arise from past events such as obtaining a loan to buy equipment for your business. These past events create an obligation that you cannot avoid. You typically transfer assets to settle liabilities. For example, when you hire employees, you promise to pay cash for their services. Hiring the employee is the past event and your promise to pay is your obligation that you cannot avoid once the employee provides the service. Issuing a paycheck is the transfer of the asset, cash. An increase in liability is credited, while a decrease is debited.

Expenses

[4] Expenses reduce assets or increase liabilities for a given period. For example, the fuel that your delivery truck consumes is an expense. When you buy gas for the truck, it reduces your cash, which is your asset. Similarly, if you buy gas using a credit card, it increases your liability. Expenses are often repeating events. For example, you must pay your vehicle leases by the same date each month. The moment you record an expense depends on the accounting basis you are using. Most businesses use the accrual basis. When you use the accrual basis, you record the expense before you pay it. The entry is to record a debit in the expense account and a credit in the liability payable account. Conversely, if you use cash-basis accounting, you record the expense only when you pay for it. In this case, you record a debit to the applicable asset account, usually cash, and a credit to the expense account.

Revenues

[5] Revenue results from sales and the delivery of services. Revenues can result in increases to assets accounts or decreases in liability accounts. Selling merchandise on a cash basis results in increasing your assets. In the same manner, selling on credit terms reduces your liabilities since the customer promises to pay you at a later date. To record increase in revenue, you debit the account and enter a credit to the account to record a reduction in revenue.

Owner's equity

[6] Equity is the money or capital that you put into your business, hence the phrase "owner's equity". Technically, equity represents all the ways in which your business draws its resources so that it functions or operates properly. Owner's equity is equal to assets minus liabilities, and this is the basic accounting equation. An increase in equity is credited, while a decrease in it is debited. Investments and revenues increase equity, while withdrawals and expenses reduce it.

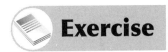 **Exercise**

Decide whether the following statements are true (T) or false (F) according to the information in Passage B.

(1) Increases in assets are in the debit column while decreases are in the credit column. (   )

(2) Each transaction is recorded either in the debit or the credit. (   )

(3) For a delivery business, credit sales mean your customers do not pay your service fees upon delivering goods. (   )

(4) As a delivery business, your assets always increase so you always debit the account. (   )

(5) To transfer assets in this paragraph means to sell assets. (   )

(6) An increase in liability means also an increase in asset; the former is credited and the latter is debited. (   )

(7) Typically the accounting basis includes the accrual one and the cash one. (   )

(8) Whether you use accrual or cash basis accounting, you record a debit in the expense account.

(9) Revenue is sure to decrease liabilities. (   )

(10) To draw its resources means to make full use of its resources. (   )

Unit

3

Assets and Liability

Asset

[1] An asset is officially defined as: A resource controlled by the enterprise as a result of past events and from which future economic benefits are expected to flow to the enterprise. To put it more simply: An asset is a possession of a business that will bring the business benefits in the future. An asset is anything that will add future value to your business.

[2] Employees can even be seen as assets. An asset is anything that will add *future value* to your business. Employees can even be seen as assets.

[3] What is the test of whether something is considered an asset for your business? Well, one asks, "Is something I own, and will it bring me benefits in the future?"

[4] Let's take land for an example. If you owned the land, would it be an asset for your business? Not sure? Well, do you expect to receive benefits for your business in the future from the land? Of course. So what are the benefits it will bring? Well, you can construct a building on it that you can use for business. Even selling it would bring benefits, in the form of cash.

[5] How about a computer that you own—is this an asset? Will it bring you benefits in the future? Well, amongst other things, you can store and retrieve large amounts of information and use it to communicate with suppliers and customers. So yes, a computer is certainly an asset.

[6] What about a motor vehicle—is this an asset? Does it have benefits for your business, and if so, what are they? Yes, there are benefits for your business... You can use the motor vehicle to pick up and deliver goods. So yes, this is also an asset.

[7] Now let's take something more tricky—what about cash? Is cash an asset? Cash is certainly an asset. What are the benefits of having cash? You can pay for things! That is certainly useful (and indeed essential) for a business.

[8] Have you ever heard of debtors? Debtors are people that owe your business money and the value of these debts as a whole.

[9] Another name for debtors is accounts receivable. The word "receivable" simply means capable of being received, or will be received.

[10] Would debtors or accounts receivable be an asset for your business? Even though you cannot own a debtor, you will get benefits in future from having money owed to your business.

[11] The benefits are simple—you will get paid! So if you have $3,000 owed to you by Mr. Smith, you have a debtor, an asset, worth $3,000.

[12] An additional requirement for an asset is that you have to be able to measure its value somehow and you have to be able to measure this accurately. This is usually quite simple, as the value is equal to how much you paid for it.

[13] So let's return to employees... How do you value an employee? Can you put an accurate, reliable figure on how much an employee is worth to you, bearing in mind that he or she can resign at any point by giving notice? Tricky, right? As you can imagine, it's nearly impossible to place a value on people—consequently employees are actually never included as assets in accounting—but only because we can't value them.

[14] So the full test of whether something is an asset is:

- Does your business own/control it?
- Will it bring your business benefits in the future?
- Can you value it accurately?

If these three criteria are met, then you have an asset according to the accounting system.

[15] There's a basic rule about how one values any asset. The rule is: The cost of an asset includes all costs necessary to get it to the business premises and into a condition in which it can be sold.

[16] So the cost of an asset can include the following:

- Purchase price;
- Import duties;
- Transport costs to get it to your premises;
- Installation or set-up costs.

Liability

[17] A liability is officially defined as: a present obligation of the enterprise arising from past events, the settlement of which is expected to result in an outflow from the enterprise of resources embodying economic benefits. In other words, a liability is simply a debt of the business. The debt will result in assets (usually cash) leaving the business in the future.

[18] Examples of liabilities: The most common liability is a loan. Another common liability is called creditors. A creditor, also known as a payable, is any business or person that you owe (apart from a loan). Suppliers (who you owe for products purchased on credit) would fall under creditors.

[19] Other examples of creditors are the telephone company that you owe or a printing shop

you owe for printing fliers. Even the tax authorities could be considered a creditor if you owe them. When you pay a loan back, or you pay off your creditors, some of your assets (most often cash) will leave your business.

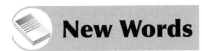 **New Words**

possession [pə'zeʃn] *n.* 占有物，所有物
retrieve [ri'tri:v] *vt.* 检索；恢复
tricky ['triki] *adj.* 微妙的；狡猾的
debtor ['detə(r)] *n.* 债务人；借方
premise ['premis] *n.* （常为*pl.*）房屋及土地

duty ['dju:ti] *n.* 税收；义务
embody [im'bɔdi] *vt.* 体现
creditor ['kreditə(r)] *n.* 债权人，债主
flier ['flaiə] *n.* （产品的）宣传单

 Special Terms

economic benefit 经济效益
import duty 进口税

transport cost 运输费用
installation or set-up cost 安装费

 **Notes**

Paras. [1] to [4]

1. ... from which future economic benefits are expected to flow to the enterprise.
   本句中的定语从句里用了 expect 的被动语态，which 代表先行词 a resource（见文中）。将本句改为主动语态来理解即 ... expect the economic benefits to flow the economic benefits to the enterprise from the resource，意为"期待这个资源产生经济效益不断流入企业"，即对应下文的 bring the business benefits "给公司带来利益"和 add future value to your business "为公司提升价值"。

2. If you owned the land, would it be an asset for your business?
   这个句子里的动词形式为虚拟语气形态，if 从句里的 own 用的是过去式，主句用了 would + 动词原形，表示与现在事实相反，是一种假设。全句的意思是：如果你拥有一块地，这能是你企业的资产吗？

Para. [5]

3. ... amongst other things, you can store and retrieve large amounts of information and use it to communicate with suppliers and customers.

本句中的 among other things 这个介词短语表示"除了其余的很多事情以外",相当于 in addition to other things 或 besides other things。全句的意思是：计算机能做的事很多，还能储存和检索大量的信息，你可以利用这些信息与供应商和客户进行沟通交流。

Paras. [8] to [10]

4. Debtors are people that owe your business money and the value of these debts as a whole.

Debtor 表示"公司债务人"，在本句中由一个定语从句修饰。your business money 和 the value of these debts as a whole 作 owe 的直接宾语。全句的意思是：债务人就是欠你公司钱的那些人，所欠债务的总值的全部债务人。

5. Even though you cannot own a debtor, you will get benefits in future from having money owed to your business.

请注意本句中 own 和 owe 的区别：own 表示"拥有"，owe 是"欠"的意思。全句的意思是：即使你没有债务人，只要有欠你公司钱的，你也能在将来获得利益。

Paras. [17] to [18]

6. ... the settlement of which is expected to result in an outflow from the enterprise of resources embodying economic benefits.

本句中定语从句里的名词短语 the settlement of... 即 settle the obligation/liability/debt，表示"解决债务，欠债还钱"；to be expected to do sth. 表示"某件事情即将发生"；result in 为"导致……的结果"。全句的意思是：解决债务问题就预示着会出现这样的结果，即体现公司经济利益的资源就要外流。

7. A creditor, also known as a payable, is any business or person that you owe (apart from a loan).

本句中的 payable 作名词用，表示"必须支付的对象"，即 creditor "债权人"。本句说明，债权人不单是放款人或放款机构，还包括欠款的任何单位和个人。

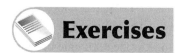 **Exercises**

Ex. 1 **Decide whether the following statements are true (T) or false (F) according to the information in Passage A.**

(1) If you own a land, even you use it not for the benefit for your business, the land is still the asset of your business. (   )

(2) Computers, motor vehicles, and cash can all bring benefits to your business, so they are all your business's assets. (   )

(3) If your customers have bought your products and they have not paid for them, they are

debtors of your business. (   )

(4) Debtors cannot be said to be the assets of your business. (   )

(5) Although something that can bring the benefits to your business, it is not an asset if you cannot measure its value. (   )

(6) Employees can be valued because you will pay them for their work. (   )

(7) The cost of an asset is just its price at which the business has purchased it. (   )

(8) Every equipment your business purchases has import duties. (   )

(9) To settle the obligation of the business means some of the assets will leave it. (   )

(10) Any suppliers are creditors of your business. (   )

Ex. 2 **Match each of the words in the box to the following phrases or definitions that is most closely related.**

A. debtor	B. receivable	C. creditor	D. flier
E. possession	F. premises	G. duty	H. loan

(1) a tax on imports (   )

(2) a piece of paper containing an advertisement or information, usually given out to people walking by (   )

(3) capable of being received (   )

(4) an entity or person that lends money or extends credit to another party (   )

(5) a house or building, together with its land and outbuildings, occupied by a business or considered in an official context (   )

(6) an item of property; something belonging to one (   )

(7) a person or an enterprise that is in debt or under financial obligation to another (   )

(8) a debt provided by an organization or individual to another entity at an interest rate (   )

Ex. 3 **Use the words mentioned in Ex. 2 to complete the following sentences. Change the form if necessary.**

(1) A _____ may file for bankruptcy, which is called "voluntary bankruptcy".

(2) _____ -free shops (or stores) are retail outlets that are exempt from the payment of certain local or national taxes and duties, on the requirement that the goods sold will be sold to travelers who will take them out of the country.

(3) We distributed _____ promoting our cleaning business.

(4) The _____ is generally provided at a cost, referred to as interest on the debt.

(5) He described the picture as his most cherished _____.

(6) Accounts _____ are treated as a current asset on a balance sheet.

(7) There is no smoking allowed anywhere on school _____.

(8) A bank is a _____ when it issues a $ 30,000 mortgage.

Ex. 4 Fill in the blanks with the words and phrases given in the box. Change the form if necessary.

| define | deliver | retrieve | value |
| resign | embody | pay off | own |

(1) The prime minister will _____ if the vote goes against him.

(2) Its constitution, actualization and management _____ the decision and volition of government to develop science and technology.

(3) The property _____ at over $2 million.

(4) No bank could ever _____ its creditors if they all demanded their money at once.

(5) Computers can instantly _____ millions of information bits.

(6) The happiest are not those who _____ all the best things, but those who can appreciate the beauty of life.

(7) The globalization _____ as the worldwide movement toward economic, financial, trade, and communications integration.

(8) We can perhaps claim compensation from the steel suppliers for failure _____ on time.

Ex. 5 Fill in the blanks with "debtor" or "creditor" in the following short passage:

A (1) _____ is a person or enterprise that owes money to another party. (The party to whom the money is owed is often a supplier or bank that will be referred to as the (2)_____.)

A (3) _____ is a person, bank, or other enterprise that has lent money or extended credit to another party. (The party to whom the credit has been granted is often a customer that will now be referred to as a (4)_____.)

If Company X borrowed money from its bank, Company X is the (5)_____ and the bank is the (6)_____. If Supplier A sold merchandise to Retailer B, then Supplier A is the (7)_____ and Retailer B is the (8)_____.

Passage B

Financial Statement—Statement of Owner's Equity

[1] Financial statements are set of accounting reports that convey economic and financial information to outside users such as creditors and investors. Four major components of financial statements are:

- balance sheet (statement of financial position);
- income statement;
- statement of owner's equity;
- statement of cash flows.

[2] Statement of owners' equity shows the changes in the equity for a period of time. Period of time is the same as the time that was covered by the income statement—often one year. Main components of equity are:

- contributed capital (common stock);
- retained earnings.

[3] Contributed capital is the investment made by owners for corporation; stock investment for sole proprietorship/partnership, whichever amount was invested into the business.

[4] Retained earning is the net income that's been earned and reinvested rather than paid out as dividends, and applyies to corporation only, not sole proprietorship/partnership.

Statement of Owner's Equity

[5] The statement of owner's equity is a financial statement that reports the changes in the equity section of the balance sheet during an accounting period. In other words, it reports the events that increased or decreased the stockholder's equity over the course of the accounting period.

[6] The statement of owner's equity is one of the shorter financial statements because there aren't many transactions that actually affect the equity accounts. It typically lists the net income or loss for the period along with the owner's contributions or withdrawals during the period.

[7] The report itself is presented in a simple equation style format like this: Beginning equity balance plus net income and owner's contributions less net loss and owner's withdrawals, ending equity balance.

[8] The ending equity account balance is always carried forward to the following year and becomes the future year's beginning balance. Obviously, the first year a business is started, it will not have a beginning balance. Let's see an example.

[9] Kaitlin's Kupcakes is a bakery in downtown Seattle that was started this year with Kaitlin's investment of $15,000. During the year, the company made a profit of $10,000 and Kaitlin decided to withdraw $5,000 from the company to pay for her living expenses. The statement of owner's equity would calculate the ending balance in the equity account of $20,000 (0 + $15,000 + $10,000 − $5,000). This ending balance will be carried forward to the following year as the future beginning balance.

[10] External users analyze this report to understand the transactions that affect the equity balance; for instance, when a creditor would like to see the amounts that Kaitlin put into her business and the amounts that she withdrew throughout the year. If Kaitlin were to keep putting money into the business, it would typically indicate that the business can't fund its own operations.

 **Exercise**

Decide whether the following statements are true (T) or false (F) according to the information in Passage B.

(1) Financial statements are made for CEO (Chief Executive Officer) of the enterprise to read. ( )

(2) Balance sheet, income statement, statement of owner's equity and statement of cash flows embody the financial position of the business. ( )

(3) The income statement covers the same period of time as that of statement of owner's equity, often one year. ( )

(4) Major components of equity are also four, as those of financial statements. ( )

(5) Earnings that are not paid out as dividends are reinvested, which are called retained earnings, which took place also in sole proprietorship/partnership. ( )

(6) The equation of the report of equity is the same of the balance sheet. ( )

(7) The equation of the statement of owner's equity is also used in a new business without any change. ( )

(8) A new business's statement of owner's equity has of course no beginning balance. ( )

(9) The retained earnings of Kaitlin's bakery are $10,000. ( )

(10) The ending balance will become the beginning balance of the next year. ( )

Unit

4

When to Recognize Revenue & Expenses

[1] Money is constantly flowing in and out of your business. How do you know when you should recognize or account for revenue? Is it during production? When you receive any form of payment? What if your clients make installments? When do you start recognizing and recording the incoming money as revenue?

[2] How about expenses? Is rent considered an expense only at the time of your monthly payment, or do you calculate this expense annually?

[3] Recognizing revenue and expenses is a timing strategy that takes some thought and effort. Here's a few things to keep in mind as you work with your accountant.

Revenue recognition principle

[4] So when do you recognize revenue in your reports, statements and forecasts? Let's start with defining the revenue recognition principle, and then we'll pick it apart.

[5] Revenue recognition principle tells that revenue is to be recognized only when the rewards and benefits associated with the items sold or service provided is transferred, where the amount can be estimated reliably and when the amount is recoverable.

[6] The textbook definition of the revenue recognition principle is: Revenue recognition generally occurs (1) when realized or realizable, and (2) when earned.

[7] A company exchanges products, merchandise, or other assets for cash or claims to cash. For example: A monthly online academic journal receives 2,000 subscriptions of $180 to be paid at the beginning of the year. Each month it recognizes revenue worth $30,000 [($180 ÷ 12) × $ 2,000].

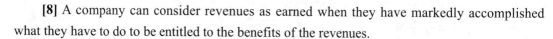

[8] A company can consider revenues as earned when they have markedly accomplished what they have to do to be entitled to the benefits of the revenues.

[9] Sales provide a verifiable measure of revenue—the sales price. If you attempt to recognize revenue before an actual sale occurs, you open the door to wide interpretations. Sales provide an objective and uniform test for revenue recognition.

Expense recognition

[10] Companies recognize expenses not when they pay wages or make a product, but when the work (service) or the product actually contributes to revenue. Thus, companies tie expense recognition to revenue recognition. That is, by matching efforts (expenses) with accomplishment (revenues), the expense recognition principle is implemented in accordance with the definition of expense (outflows or other using up of assets or incurring of liabilities).

Why you need to know about revenue and expense recognition

[11] Often, a business will spend cash on producing their goods before it is sold or will receive cash for goods it has not yet delivered. Without the matching principle and the recognition rules, a business would be forced to record revenues and expenses when it received or paid cash. This could distort a business's income statement and make it look like they were doing much better or much worse than is actually the case. By tying revenues and expenses to the completion of sales and other money generating tasks, the income statement will better reflect what happened in terms of what revenue and expense generating activities during the accounting period.

[12] You want your reports and statements to be as accurate and as transparent as possible. Making sure you've recognized revenue and expenses at the right times will help you grow your business as you look for investors and satisfy shareholders.

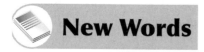 **New Words**

---

claim [kleim] *vt. & vi.* 声称；索取　*n.* 声称；索赔

distort [di'stɔːt] *vt. & vi.* 歪曲，扭曲

estimate ['estimət] *vt.* 判断；估计

implement ['implimənt] *vt.* 实施，执行；使生效

incur [in'kɜː(r)] *vt.* 使发生；招致，引起；遭受

installment [in'stɔːlmənt] *n.* 分期付款

intermediate [ˌintə'miːdiət] *adj.* 中级的

interpretation [inˌtəːpri'teiʃn] *n.* 解释，说明

markedly ['mɑːkidli] *adv.* 显著地，引人注目地

merchandise ['mɜːtʃəndais] *n.* 商品，货物　*vt. & vi.* 买卖，销售；经商

realizable ['riːəlaizəbl] *adj.* 可实现的，可实行的

realized ['riəˌlaizd] *adj.* 实现的

---

recoverable [ri'kʌvərəbl] *adj.* 可收回的；可重获的	transfer [træns'fə:(r)] *vt.* 使转移，使调动，转让（权利等）
reliably [ri'laiəbli] *adv.* 可靠地，确实地	uniform ['ju:nifɔ:m] *adj.* 规格一致的，一样的
subscription [səb'skripʃn] *n.*（报刊等的）订阅费	verifiable ['verifaiəbl] *adj.* 能作证的，能证实的

Special Terms

academic journal 学术期刊	revenue recognition 收入确认
expense recognition 费用确认	rewards and benefits 待遇和利益
realized revenue 已实现收入	timing strategy 择时策略

Notes

Para. [1]

1. How do you know when you should recognize or account for revenue?

   本句中的 account for 可理解为 provide a reckoning of (expenditure, payments, income, etc.)"确认（花费、支付、收入等）"，即下文的 recording the incoming money as revenue "确认收入 / 将其列入收入"。

2. What if your clients make installments?

   What 后边省略了 will/would you do。全句的意思是：如果客户采用分期付款方式，你何时确认收入入账呢？

Paras. [4] to [5]

3. Let's start with defining the revenue recognition principle, and then we'll pick it apart.

   动词短语 pick it apart 的原意是"分开，解剖"，这里表达的意思是"仔细分析"。

4. ... only when the rewards and benefits associated with the items sold or service provided is transferred...

   本句用了 only when 表示只有在这个时间段内的收入才能被确认；the rewards and benefits associated with the items sold 指"与收益相关的项目已经出售"；短语 service provided is transferred 中的 transfer 等同于 deliver，指"与收益相关的服务已经完成"。

5. ... where the amount can be estimated reliably and when the amount is recoverable.

   本句中 where 分句中的 the amount 指前文中提到的收益，表示"收益数额能够确切地估算"；and 连接的 when 分句和 where 分句并列，表示只有在这个数额可以收回的时候。

Para. [8]

6. A company can consider revenues as earned when they have markedly accomplished what they have to do to be entitled to the benefits of the revenues.

本句中 when 分句中的主语 they 指代 revenues；have markedly accomplished what they have to do 指"毫无争议地完成了它们必须做的事情"；to be entitled to the benefits of the revenues 指"有资格被叫作收益"，也可以理解为"能够确认是收益的才算是收入"。

Para. [10]

7. Companies recognize expenses not when they pay wages or make a product, but when the work (service) or the product actually contributes to revenue.

本句中的 not when they pay wages or make a product 和 actually contributes to revenue 表示（开支的确认）不是在支付工资或者生产一个产品的时候，而是在提供劳务或者销售产品实实在在地产生收入的时候。本句强调开支必须匹配效益。

Para. [11]

8. ... make it look like they were doing much better or much worse than is actually the case.

look like 即 It seems likely that...，指"很可能出现或引起某事或做某事"。本句的意思是：这可能导致报表比公司的实际运行状况要好得多或者糟糕得多。

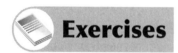

Exercises

Ex. 1 Decide whether the following statements are true (T) or false (F) according to the information in Passage A.

(1) When to recognize and record the incoming money as revenue is not a problem worth discussing. (   )
(2) When to calculate the expenses just like when to record the revenue is the problem this article is dealing with. (   )
(3) Revenue recognition principle stipulates when you receive any form of payment, revenue should be recognized. (   )
(4) In "service provided is transferred", "transferred" can be replaced by "delivered". (   )
(5) At the beginning of the year, the online journal receives $360,000 subscriptions, which can be recognized as its revenues. (   )
(6) Revenues realized are sure to be earned. (   )
(7) Revenue recognition can be only objectively tested by sales. (   )
(8) When companies pay employees wages or make products, expenses are recognized. (   )

(9) In order to guarantee the company's accurate and transparent reports and statements, make sure to recognize revenues and expenses at the right time. (   )

(10) Outsiders have nothing to do with the company's report and statement. (   )

Ex. 2 Match each of the words in the box to the following phrases or definitions that is most closely related.

A. installment	B. recoverable	C. realizable	D. merchandise
E. claim	F. subscription	G. verifiable	H. transparent

(1) goods that are bought and sold

(2) a statement saying that you have a right to something

(3) an amount of money that you pay regularly to receive a product or service

(4) one of the parts into which a debt is divided when payment is made at intervals

(5) open and honest, without secrets

(6) able to be proved

(7) able to be sold to get money

(8) able to be regained or retrieved

Ex. 3 Use the words mentioned in Ex. 2 to complete the following sentences. Change the form if necessary.

(1) The receivables, therefore, are not stated at estimated net _____ value.

(2) The reputation of the firm was blown upon for passing substandard products off as first-class _____.

(3) Your business can be listed on the website for a low monthly _____.

(4) Companies need to be _____ about their goals and policies.

(5) They sought to demonstrate that the electoral process was neither accountable nor transparent and its results are, therefore, non- _____.

(6) Buying goods on the _____ plan has become epidemic in recent years.

(7) Removal expenses might be _____ if you have to move to a different area in order to find work.

(8) International arrivals go to immigration and baggage _____ on the first floor.

Ex. 4 Fill in the blanks with the words and phrase given in the box. Change the form if necessary.

break down	recognize	calculate	incur
transfer	exchange	accomplish	distort

(1) The boy's parents promised _____ one hundred dollars to his bank account every month while he was away at college.

(2) Many institutions _____ information by hand because of incompatible computer systems.

(3) The developed world should be serious about removing subsidies which _____ trade and which damage the environment.

(4) The new data team set out _____ the goals laid out by the supervisor and they operated with enthusiasm.

(5) Let's _____ the project into smaller parts in order to deal with them one by one.

(6) Accounting on an accrual basis is intended to match up revenue and expenses when they _____ or delivered, without regard to when payment is issued or received.

(7) Revenue recognition is an accounting principle under GAAP that determines the specific conditions under which revenue _____ or accounted for.

(8) They also _____ the cost savings emerging from the amount of disease that would be avoided because of lower blood pressure.

Ex. 5 Translate the following short passage into Chinese.

Recoverable Amount

In simple terms, the recoverable amount is the highest value that can be obtained from an asset. We can think of two general ways we can obtain value from an asset: (a) from using that asset in the business or (b) by selling it to someone else. The value of (a) is the present value of expected future cash flows from using the asset. The value of (b) is the fair value of the asset less costs to sell the asset. The higher amount from these two alternatives is the recoverable amount.

The recoverable amount is used in the test for impairment (the state of being diminished, weakened, or damaged). The reason that the recoverable amount is the higher figure from the two alternative estimates is that we presume that the company's management will choose the best (value-maximizing) option.

There are complications when the asset in question must be used in combination with other assets to generate identifiable cash flows. If this is the case, then the recoverable amount must be determined for this group of assets, called a "cash generating unit".

Passage B

Differences Between Cash Basis and Accrual Basis Accounting

[1] Choosing the appropriate accounting method for your business is an important decision that will ultimately direct everything from financial reporting to tax filings. In the early stages of a small business, the cash basis is often the "go-to" method of accounting whereas more complex or larger businesses with over a million or more in annual revenue use the accrual basis—however, the reasons for a given choice can vary based on business size and needs.

[2] In fact, choosing the right method for your business requires some consideration.

What is cash basis accounting

[3] The cash basis accounting method is the system used by most people for their personal finances, such as keeping track of the balance in their checking accounts. Cash basis accounting records income and expenses at the time that the transaction occurs. With a personal checking account, deposits (revenue) are added to the balance when funds are received, while checks (expenses) are deducted when they are written. Cash basis accounting for a business works in a similar manner. Sales are recorded when the payment is received and expenses are recorded when paid, all without regard to when services are delivered or expenses are incurred. In simplest terms, cash basis accounting is based on when the money changes hands.

What is accrual basis accounting

[4] Accounting on an accrual basis is intended to match up revenue and expenses when they are incurred or delivered, without regard to when payment is issued or received.

[5] This is markedly different because it aims to correlate expenses and revenue to help give a greater measure of profitability and business health. Some examples of this include:

[6] Your customer places an order for $1,000 and you ship the product, allowing him 30 days to pay for the order. You would record the sales in the current period, with the offsetting entry to the accounts receivable section on the balance sheet. When you receive the payment from the customer, you would not need to record sales; instead, the entries would be to cash and accounts receivable.

[7] You receive a utility bill on June 30 for June utilities, but you do not plan to pay it until July 10. Before closing your books for June, you would accrue the liability by posting an entry to debit utility expenses and credit accounts payable. In July, you would mark the bill in accounts payable as paid.

[8] You renew an annual software license for $1,200 in the month of January. However, instead of recording an expense of $1,200 for January, the expense is expensed over the entire year at $100 per month.

What are the advantages and disadvantages of each

[9] The cash method of accounting is the simplest method and the method that is most familiar to the majority of people. It also gives you the best picture of how much cash you truly have available for operating your business. However, it can offer a biased picture of your profit and loss as revenue and expenses are often recognized in different periods. For example, suppose you spend $2,000 on June 25 to purchase products to fill a customer's order, your customer picks up his order on July 1 and pays you $3,000. In the unlikely event that you had no other transactions for either month, your income statement would show a loss of $2,000 in June and a profit of $3,000 in July.

[10] The accrual method of accounting does a better job of matching income and expenses to the appropriate period. This gives you a better picture of your true profit or loss. However,

the accrual method tends to obscure your view of how much operating cash you actually have available, so you might need to prepare frequent cash flow statements to get a better picture. The accrual method is also more complicated and time-consuming to execute, often requiring the support of accounting professionals to execute and analyze.

Can I choose either method

[11] Anyone can choose to use the accrual method of accounting, but the IRS has rules for who can use the cash method.

[12] The company's operates as a C corporation and has gross receipts that average more than $5 million per year for the most recent three years.

[13] You cannot meet the IRS definition of a tax shelter.

[14] If you maintain an inventory, you must use the accrual method to record your inventory purchases and sales, but you can use the cash method for other revenue and expenses, such as rent or interest income.

Which method should I choose

[15] The choice of an accounting method depends on a number of factors, such as the size of your business, your comfort level with accounting procedures and the nature of your business. If you are a one-person fledgling operation, your needs will not be the same as an established manufacturing concern with 100 employees. However, keep in mind that if you maintain an inventory, you will need to use the accrual method to record part of your entries, and when your business exceeds the gross receipts limit, the IRS will likely force you to convert completely to accrual basis accounting. You might find it easier to dive into the accrual method from the start rather than use a "hybrid" method or be faced with radical changes in the future.

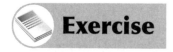 **Exercise**

Decide whether the following statements are true (T) or false (F) according to the information in Passage B.

(1) No doubt, small businesses will use the cash basis accounting. (　　)

(2) Whether you choose the cash or the accrual method of accounting has nothing to do with the size of your business. (　　)

(3) Common people do not use neither of the two methods, cash or accrual basis one, for their personal finance. (　　)

(4) Cash basis accounting also needs to regard to when services are delivered or expenses are incurred. (　　)

(5) When you receive the payment from the customer, it's time you should record sales if you use the accrual method of accounting. (　　)

(6) The cash method of accounting can provide you with an objective picture of your profit and loss. (　　)

(7) To record an inventory, you have no choice but to use the accrual method of accounting. (　　)

(8) The large corporation like a C corp has to use the accrual method of accounting. (　　)

(9) It's not difficult to change the accounting method from the cash basis to the accrual one. (　　)

(10) That an S corporation is kind of like the lite version of a C corporation indicates that typically it is much smaller than a C corporation. (　　)

Unit 5

Balance Sheet

Balance sheet

[1] A balance sheet reports a company's assets, liabilities and shareholders' equity at a specific point in time, and provides a basis for computing rates of return and evaluating its capital structure. It is a financial statement that provides a snapshot of what a company owns and owes, as well as the amount invested by shareholders.

Breaking down balance sheet

[2] The balance sheet adheres to the following equation, where assets on one side, and liabilities plus shareholders' equity on the other, balance out: Assets = Liabilities + Shareholders' Equity.

[3] This is intuitive: A company has to pay for all the things it owns (assets) by either borrowing money (taking on liabilities) or taking it from investors (issuing shareholders' equity).

[4] For example, if a company takes out a five-year, $4,000 loan from a bank, its assets—specifically the cash account—will increase by $4,000; its liabilities—specifically the long-term debt account—will also increase by $4,000, balancing the two sides of the equation. If the company takes $8,000 from investors, its assets will increase by that amount, as will its shareholders' equity. All revenues the company generates in excess of its liabilities will go into the shareholders' equity account, representing the net assets held by the owners. These revenues will be balanced on the assets side, appearing as cash, investments, inventory, or some other asset.

[5] Assets, liabilities and shareholders' equity are each comprised of several smaller accounts that break down the specifics of a company's finances. These accounts vary widely by industry,

and the same terms can have different implications depending on the nature of the business. Broadly, however, there are a few common components investors are likely to come across.

Assets

[6] Within the assets segment, accounts are listed from top to bottom in order of their liquidity, that is, the ease with which they can be converted into cash. They are divided into current assets, those which can be converted to cash in one year or less; and non-current or long-term assets, which cannot.

[7] Here is the general order of accounts within current assets:

- Cash and cash equivalents: the most liquid assets, these can include Treasury bills and short-term certificates of deposit, as well as hard currency;
- Marketable securities: equity and debt securities for which there is a liquid market;
- Accounts receivable: money which customers owe the company, perhaps including an allowance for doubtful accounts (an example of a contra account), since a certain proportion of customers can be expected not to pay;
- Inventory: goods available for sale, valued at the lower of the cost or market price;
- Prepaid expenses: representing value that has already been paid for, such as insurance, advertising contracts or rent.

[8] Long-term assets include the following:

- Long-term investments: securities that will not or cannot be liquidated in the next year;
- Fixed assets: these include land, machinery, equipment, buildings and other durable, generally capital-intensive assets;
- Intangible assets: these include non-physical, but still valuable, assets such as intellectual property and goodwill; in general, intangible assets are only listed on the balance sheet if they are acquired, rather than developed in-house; their value may, therefore, be wildly understated—by not including a globally recognized logo, for example—or just as wildly overstated.

Liabilities

[9] Liabilities are the money that a company owes to outside parties, from bills it has to pay to suppliers, to interest on bonds it has issued to creditors, to rent, utilities and salaries. Current liabilities are those that are due within one year and are listed in order of their due date. Long-term liabilities are due at any point after one year.

[10] Current liabilities accounts might include:

- Current portion of long-term debt;
- Bank indebtedness;
- Interest payable;
- Rent, tax, utilities;
- Wages payable;

- Customer prepayments;
- Dividends payable and others.

[11] Long-term liabilities can include:

- Long-term debt: interest and principal on bonds issued;
- Pension fund liability: the money a company is required to pay into its employees' retirement accounts;
- Deferred tax liability: taxes that have been accrued but will not be paid for another year; besides timing, this figure reconciles differences between requirements for financial reporting and the way tax is assessed, such as depreciation calculations;
- Some liabilities are off-balance sheet, meaning that they will not appear on the balance sheet. Operating leases are an example of this kind of liability.

Shareholders' equity

[12] Shareholders' equity is the money attributable to a business's owners, meaning its shareholders. It is also known as "net assets", since it is equivalent to the total assets of a company minus its liabilities, that is, the debt it owes to non-shareholders.

[13] Retained earnings are the net earnings a company either reinvests in the business or uses to pay off debt; the rest is distributed to shareholders in the form of dividends.

[14] Treasury stock is the stock a company has either repurchased or never issued in the first place. It can be sold at a later date to raise cash or reserved to repel a hostile takeover.

[15] Some companies issue preferred stock, which will be listed separately from common stock under shareholders' equity. Each year, the holders of the preferred stock are to receive their dividends before the common stockholders. In exchange for this preferential treatment for dividends, the preferred stockholders (or shareholders) generally will never receive more than the stated dividend.

[16] Additional paid-in capital or capital surplus represents the amount shareholders have invested in excess of the "common stock" or "preferred stock" accounts, which are based on par value rather than market price. Shareholders' equity is not directly related to a company's market capitalization: the latter is based on the current price of a stock, while paid-in capital is the sum of the equity that has been purchased at any price.

How to interpret a balance sheet

[17] The balance sheet is a snapshot, representing the state of a company's finances at a moment in time. By itself, it cannot give a sense of the trends that are playing out over a longer period. For this reason, the balance sheet should be compared with those of previous periods. It should also be compared with those of other businesses in the same industry, since different industries have unique approaches to financing.

[18] A number of ratios can be derived from the balance sheet, helping investors get a sense of how healthy a company is. These include the debt-to-equity ratio and the acid-test ratio, along with many others. The income statement and statement of cash flows also provide valuable context for assessing a company's finances, as do any notes or addenda in an earnings report that might refer back to the balance sheet.

New Words

accrue [ə'kru:] vt. & vi. 应计；增加；累积

addenda [ə'dendə] n. 补遗，附录（addendum 的复数）

allowance [ə'lauəns] n. 折扣；津贴，补贴；限额

analyst ['ænəlist] n. 分析者，分析家

arbitrary ['ɑ:bitrəri] adj. 随意的，任性的

attributable [ə'tribjətəbl] adj. 有归属的

capital-intensive [ˌkæpitl-in'tensiv] adj. 资金密集型的

capitalization [ˌkæpitəlai'zeiʃn] n. 资本化

contra ['kɔntrə] n. 备抵；反对，相反

defer [di'fə:(r)] vt.（使）推迟，（使）延期

depreciation [diˌpri:ʃi'eiʃn] n.（资产等）折旧；货币贬值

dividend ['dividend] n. 红利，股息

goodwill [ˌgud'wil] n.（企业的）信誉，声誉，商誉

indebt [in'det] vt. 使负债

indebtedness [in'detidnəs] n. 亏欠，债务

intangible [in'tændʒəbl] adj. 无形的

intuitive [in'tju:itiv] adj. 直觉的，凭直觉获知的；直观的

investopedia [invest'pediə] n. (investment + encyclopedia) 投资百科

liquidate ['likwideit] vt. 使变现；清偿

logo ['ləugəu/'lɔgəu] n.（某公司或机构的）标识，标志

non-physical ['nɔn-'fizikl] adj. 非实体的

overstate [ˌəuvə'steit] vt. 高估

par [pɑ:(r)] n. 票面价值

pension ['penʃn] n. 退休金，养老金

preferred [pri'fə:d] adj. 首选的

principal ['prinsəpl] n. 本金

pro forma [ˌprəu 'fɔ:mə] adj. 估计的

reconcile ['rekənsail] vt. 核对；使和好，使和解

repel [ri'pel] vt. 击退；抵制

security [si'kjuərəti] n. 有价证券

segment ['segmənt] n. 部分，段落

shareholder ['ʃeəhəuldə(r)] n. 股东；股票持有者

snapshot ['snæpʃɔt] n.（快照）照片

specific [spə'sifik] n. 详情，细节；特性

takeover ['teikəuvə(r)] n. 接管；（经营权等的）收购

treasury ['treʒəri] n. 国库；库存

understate [ˌʌndə'steit] vt. 低估

utilities [ju:'tilitiz] n. 公用事业设备（utility 的复数）

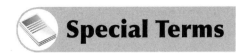 **Special Terms**

acid-test ratio (quick ratio) 酸性测试比率
（速动比率），流动比率

additional paid-in capital 股本溢价

bank indebtedness 银行负债

cash equivalents 现金等价物

common components 共同成分

contra account 备抵账户，抵消科目

current asset 流动资产，短期可以兑现的
资产

current liability 短期负债，流动负债

deferred tax liability 递延税项负债

depreciation calculation 折旧计算

doubtful account 存疑账户

financial modeling technique 金融建模技术

hard currency 硬通货

intangible asset 无形资产

intellectual property 知识产权

liquid market 流动性市场

long-term liability 长期负债

marketable security 流通证券

operating lease 经营租赁

par value 票面价值

pension fund 养老金基金

preferred stock 优先股

rate of return 收益率

treasury bill 短期政府证券

treasury stock 国库股票

 **Notes**

Para. [1]

1. ... provides a basis for computing rates of return and evaluating its capital structure.

provide a basis for 指"为某事提供依据"，即为计算公司的收益率和评估其资本结构提供依据。

Para. [5]

2. Broadly, however, there are a few common components investors are likely to come across.

a few common components 就是本句后文提到的"分解的资产、债务和权益的下属项目"；investors are likely to come across 是一个定语从句，表示"投资人通常可能碰到的这些项目"。

Paras. [6] to [8]

3. Within the assets segment, accounts are listed from top to bottom in order of their liquidity, that is, the ease with which they can be converted into cash.

assets segment 指的是"将资产按其兑现的难易程度从顶部到底部的分段"；the ease 表示"容易度"（with ease 表示"轻松"）；covert into cash 指"将资产转换成现金"。

4. ... money which customers owe the company, perhaps including an allowance for doubtful accounts (an example of a contra account)...

allowance for doubtful accounts 指 "坏账准备金"；contra account 指 "备抵账户"。这两类都附属于 accounts receivable "应收账户"。本句的意思是：客户拖欠的资金归为短期可以兑现的资产，但欠款有风险。

5. ... in general, intangible assets are only listed on the balance sheet if they are acquired, rather than developed in-house.

本句中的 rather than 表示否定，全句的意思是：通常，无形资产只有在获取利益时才会在资产负债表中列示，而不是还在内部开发。

Paras. [9] to [11]

6. Liabilities are the money that a company owes to outside parties, from bills it has to pay to suppliers, to interest on bonds it has issued to creditors, to rent, utilities and salaries.

本句用 from... to... 罗列说明了公司的外债：bills it has to pay to suppliers 指 "必须支付给供应商的账单"，interest on bonds it has issued to creditors 指 "必须支付给债权人的债券利息"，以及 to rent, utilities and salaries 指 "必须支付的租金、水电燃气等公共设施的费用以及人员薪水"。

7. ... besides timing, this figure reconciles differences between requirements for financial reporting and the way tax is assessed, such as depreciation calculations

本句描述的是：除了时间上的协调，递延所得税的数字和财务报表的要求和税务部门的估算方法存在差异，如折旧的计算问题等也必须进行调整。

Para. [12]

8. ... its liabilities, that is, the debt it owes to non-shareholders.

本句中的 liabilities 后面是一个由 that is 引导的同位语 the debt，后面有一个定语从句对其进行定义，指 "公司欠的非股东的债务"。

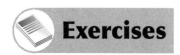 **Exercises**

Ex. 1 Decide whether the following statements are true (T) or false (F) according to the information in the passage.

(1) In "provides a basis for computing rates of return", "computing" means to use a computer to prepare a balance sheet. (   )

(2) In "what a company owns and owes" means the equity and liabilities of a company. (   )

(3) The loan increases the company's liability, but decreases its assets. (   )

(4) Assets, liabilities and shareholders' equity are each comprised of several smaller accounts, which are components of all businesses. (   )

(5) Cash and cash equivalents are the most liquid assets, meaning they are cash themselves or can be converted to cash with ease. (   )

(6) Marketable securities can be readily sold on a liquid market, such as a stock exchange or bond exchange. (   )

(7) Long-term assets are also known as noncurrent assets. (   )

(8) Fixed assets can also be converted into cash with ease. (   )

(9) Liabilities fall into two kinds, namely current ones and long-term ones. (   )

(10) Retained earnings are the net earnings after dividends that are available for reinvestment in the company's core business or to pay down its debt. (   )

Ex. 2 **Match each of the in the box words to the following phrases or definitions that is most closely related.**

A. depreciation	B. dividend	C. intangible	D. pension
E. principal	F. shareholder	G. utility	H. liquidity

(1) unable to be touched or grasped; not having physical presence

(2) a type of retirement plan that provides monthly income in retirement

(3) the original amount of money lent, not including profits and interest

(4) an owner of shares in a company

(5) a reduction in the value of an asset with the passage of time

(6) the set of services provided by the public organizations consumed by the public: electricity, natural gas, water, sewage, telephone, and transportation

(7) the availability of liquid assets to a market or company

(8) a sum of money paid regularly (typically quarterly) by a company to its shareholders out of its profits (or reserves)

Ex. 3 **Use the words mentioned in Ex. 2 to complete the following sentences. Change the form if necessary.**

(1) _____ plans must follow specific rules set out by the Department of Labor.

(2) _____ assets include goodwill, patents, trademarks, copyrights, and franchise.

(3) _____ bills usually refer to your water, electricity and gas bills.

(4) _____ can be issued as cash payments, as shares of stock, or other property.

(5) Cash is considered the standard for _____, because it can most quickly and easily be converted into other assets.

(6) If the company does poorly, _____ can lose money if the price of its stock declines.

(7) _____ is an income tax deduction that allows a taxpayer to recover the cost or other basis of certain property.

(8) The amount of interest one pays on a loan is determined by the _____ sum.

Ex. 4 Fill in the blanks with the verbs given below. Change the form if necessary.

adhere	comprise	liquidate	defer
distribute	repel	indebt	overstate

(1) Customers often _____ payment for as long as possible.

(2) They have fifty thousand troops along the border ready _____ any attack.

(3) Don't _____ your case or no one will believe you.

(4) We will _____ to strict sales ethics, with none of the cold calling that has given the industry such a bad name.

(5) Therefore net cash balances _____ cash and cash equivalents together with money market deposits.

(6) Farmers buy tools and thus _____ themselves to the tradesmen who supply these, and the debt is paid with a portion of the crop yield each harvest.

(7) And the business will have less money _____ as dividends.

(8) I had to _____ my holdings to pay off my ex-husband.

Ex. 5 Read the short passage below and then complete the multiple choices.

What Is the Acid-Test Ratio

The acid-test ratio is similar to the current ratio except that inventory, supplies, and prepaid expenses are excluded. The current ratio is a liquidity ratio that measures a company's ability to pay short-term and long-term obligations.

In other words, the acid-test ratio compares the total of the cash, temporary marketable securities, and accounts receivable to the amount of current liabilities.

Let's illustrate the acid-test ratio by assuming that a company has cash of $7,000 + temporary marketable securities of $20,000 + accounts receivables of $93,000. This adds up to $120,000 of quick assets. If its current liabilities amount to $100,000, its acid-test ratio is 1.2 ：1.

The larger the acid-test ratio, the more easily the company will be able to meet its current obligations.

The acid-test ratio is also known as the quick ratio.

(1) Which of the following statements is FALSE?

A. The acid-test ratio is somewhat different from the current ratio.

B. Inventory, supplies, and prepaid expenses can be regarded as quick assets when you calculate the current ratio.

C. Inventory, supplies, and prepaid expenses can be regarded as quick assets when you execute the acid-test ratio.

D. The formula of the acid-test ratio is a fraction, whose numerator is the company's quick assets and denominator is its amount of current liabilities.

(2) Quick assets _____.

    A. mean all assets of a company

    B. include liabilities

    C. include inventory, supplies, and prepaid expenses

    D. are assets that can be converted to cash quickly

(3) Examples of current liabilities are the following ones except _____.

    A. accounts payable   B. dividends payable

    C. long-term debts   D. interests payable

(4) The larger acid-test ratio means _____.

    A. the company is more able to pay for its current debt

    B. the company is less able to meet its current obligation

    C. the company will lose its investors

    D. the company's financial position is worse and worse

(5) Which of the following statements is FALSE?

    A. The acid-test ration reflects the company's ability to meet only the current obligations.

    B. The current ration reflects the company's ability to meet the current obligations.

    C. Inventory, supplies, and prepaid expenses don't belong to quick assets.

    D. Inventory, supplies, and prepaid expenses are quick assets.

Passage B

On Which Financial Statements Does a Company Report Its Long-Term Debt

[1] A company lists its long-term debt on its balance sheet under liabilities, usually under a subheading for long-term liabilities.

Long-term liabilities

[2] Any obligations a company bears for a time period that extends past the current operating cycle or current year are considered long-term liabilities. Long-term liabilities can be financing-related or operational. Financing liabilities are debt obligations produced when a company raises cash. They include convertible bonds, notes payable and bonds payable. Operating liabilities are obligations a company incurs during the process of conducting its normal business practices. Operating liabilities include capital lease obligations and post-retirement benefit obligations to employees.

[3] Both types of liabilities represent financial obligations a company must meet in the future, though it is advisable for investors to look at the two separately. Financing liabilities result from deliberate funding choices, providing insight into the company's capital structure and clues to future earning potential.

Long-term debt

[4] Long-term debt is listed under long-term liabilities on a company's balance sheet. Any financial obligation that involves repayment over a time period greater than 12 months is considered long-term debt. Included among these obligations are such things as long-term leases, traditional business financing loans and company bond issues.

Financial statements

[5] Financial statements record the various inflows and outflows of capital for a business. These documents present financial data about a company efficiently and allow analysts and investors to assess a company's overall profitability and financial health. To maintain continuity, financial statements are prepared in compliance with generally accepted accounting principles, or GAAP. Among the various financial statements a company regularly publishes are balance sheets, income statements and statements of retained earnings and cash flows.

Balance sheet

[6] A balance sheet is the summary of a company's liabilities, assets and shareholders' equity at a specific point in time. The three segments of the balance sheet help investors understand the amount invested into the company by shareholders, along with the company's current assets and obligations. There are a variety of accounts within each of the three segments, along with documentation of their respective values. The most important lines recorded on the balance sheet include cash, current assets, long-term assets, current liabilities, debt, long-term liabilities and shareholders' equity.

Debt versus equity

[7] A company's long-term debt, combined with specified short-term debt and preferred and common stock equity, make up its capital structure. Capital structure refers to a company's use of varied funding sources to finance operations and growth. The use of debt as a funding source is relatively less expensive than equity funding for two principal reasons. First, debtors have prior claim in the event a company goes bankrupt, thus debt is safer and commands a smaller return. This effectively means a lower interest rate for the company than that expected from the total shareholder return, or TSR, on equity. The second reason debt is less expensive as a funding source stems from the fact that interest payments are tax deductible, thus reducing the net cost of borrowing.

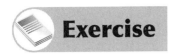

Exercise

Decide whether the following statements are true (T) or false (F) according to the information in Passage B.

(1) A company's balance sheet is comprised of assets, liabilities and equity, whether current or long-term debt is listed under liabilities. (   )

(2) Typically an operating cycle is a year, so long-term liabilities are to be paid back at least one year later. (   )

(3) Both types of liabilities refer to financial liabilities and operating ones. (   )

(4) Financial liabilities refer to the debt the company issued—often in a prior period—in exchange for cash and must repay the principal plus interest. (   )

(5) Long-term liabilities are not due within the next 12 months. (   )

(6) The financial statements comprise four basic reports: income statement, balance sheet, statement of cash flows, and statement of retained earnings. (   )

(7) The three segments of the balance sheet are liabilities, assets and shareholders' equity. (   )

(8) The company prefers using equity funding rather than the debt. (   )

(9) The total shareholder return, or TSR, on equity is much higher than the interest rate of the debt. (   )

(10) The total shareholder return, on equity is also tax deductible. (   )

Unit 6

Double Entry Accounting

Double entry accounting overview

[1] Double entry accounting is a record keeping system under which every transaction is recorded in at least two accounts. There is no limit on the number of accounts that may be used in a transaction, but the minimum is two accounts. There are two columns in each account, with debit entries on the left and credit entries on the right. In double entry accounting, the total of all debit entries must match the total of all credit entries. When this happens, the transaction is said to be "in balance". If the totals do not agree, the transaction is said to be "out of balance", and you will not be able to use the resulting information to create financial statements.

Double entry accounting definitions

[2] The definitions of a debit and credit are:

- A debit is that portion of an accounting entry that either increases an asset or expense account, or decreases a liability or equity account. It is positioned to the left in an accounting entry.

- A credit is that portion of an accounting entry that either increases a liability or equity account, or decreases an asset or expense account. It is positioned to the right in an accounting entry.

[3] An account is a separate, detailed record associated with a specific asset, liability, equity, revenue, expense, gain, or loss. Examples of accounts are:

- Cash (asset account: normally a debit balance);
- Accounts receivable (asset account: normally a debit balance);
- Inventory (asset account: normally a debit balance);

- Fixed assets (asset account: normally a debit balance);
- Accounts payable (liability account: normally a credit balance);
- Accrued liabilities (liability account: normally a credit balance);
- Notes payable (liability account: normally a credit balance);
- Common stock (equity account: normally a credit balance);
- Retained earnings (equity account: normally a credit balance);
- Revenue-products (revenue account: normally a credit balance);
- Revenue-services (revenue account: normally a credit balance);
- Cost of goods sold (expense account: normally a debit balance);
- Wage expense (expense account: normally a debit balance);
- Utilities (expense account: normally a debit balance);
- Travel and entertainment (expense account: normally a debit balance);
- Gain on sale of asset (gain account: normally a credit balance);
- Loss on sale of asset (loss account: normally a debit balance).

Double entry accounting examples

[4] Here are the double entry accounting entries associated with a variety of business transactions:

- *Buy merchandise*. You buy $1,000 of goods with the intention of later selling them to a third party. The entry is a debit to the inventory (asset) account and a credit to the cash (asset) account. In this case, you are swapping one asset (cash) for another asset (inventory).
- *Sell goods*. You sell the goods to a buyer for $1,500. There are two entries in this situation. One is a debit to the accounts receivable account for $1,500 and a credit to the revenue account for $1,500. This means that you are recording revenue while also recording an asset (accounts receivable) which represents the amount that the customer now owes you. The second entry is a $1,000 debit to the cost of goods sold (expense) account and a credit in the same amount to the inventory (asset) account. This records the elimination of the inventory asset as we charge it to expense. When netted together, the cost of goods sold of $1,000 and the revenue of $1,500 result in a profit of $500.
- *Pay employees*. You pay employees $5,000. This is a debit to the wage (expense) account and a credit to the cash (asset) account. This means that you are consuming the cash asset by paying employees.
- *Buy a fixed asset*. You pay a supplier $4,000 for a machine. The entry is a debit of $4,000 to the fixed assets (asset) account and a credit of $4,000 to the cash (asset) account. In this case, you are swapping one asset (cash) for another asset (inventory).
- *Incur debt*. You borrow $10,000 from the bank. The entry is a debit of $10,000 to the cash (asset) account and a credit of $10,000 to the notes payable (liability) account. Thus, you are incurring a liability in order to obtain cash.

- *Sell shares.* You sell $8,000 of shares to investors. The entry is a debit of $8,000 to the cash (asset) account and a credit of $8,000 to the common stock (equity) account.
- *Pay a credit card statement.* You pay a credit card statement in the amount of $6,000, and all of the purchases are for expenses. The entry is a total of $6,000 debited to several expense accounts and $6,000 credited to the cash (asset) account. Thus, you are consuming an asset by paying for various expenses.

[5] Thus, the key point with double entry accounting is that a single transaction always triggers a recordation in at least two accounts, as assets and liabilities gradually flow through a business and are converted into revenues, expenses, gains, and losses.

Alternatives to double entry accounting

[6] A simpler version of accounting is single entry accounting, which is essentially a cash basis system that is run from a check book. Under this approach, assets and liabilities are not formally tracked, which means that no balance sheet can be constructed.

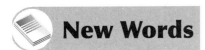 **New Words**

accrued [ə'kʊd] *adj.* 权责已发生的，应计的

alternative [ɔ:l'tə:nətiv] *n.* 可供选择的事物　*adj.* 替代的，可供选择的

convert [kən'və:t] *vt. & vi.* （使）转变，（使）转换

debit ['debit] *n.* 借方，借方账目　*vt.* 记入借方

elimination [i,limɪ'neiʃn] *n.* 排除，除去

gain [gein] *n.* 利润；获益

net [net] *n.* 网，网状织物，球网；网罩　*vt.* 净赚；捕获　*adj.* 净的，净得的

recordation [,rekə'deiʃn] *n.* 记载，记录

swap [swɔp] *vt. & vi.* 用……替换，把……换成　*n.* 交换，交换物

trigger['trigə(r)] *vt.* 引发，触发

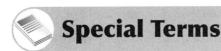 **Special Terms**

accounting entry　会计分录
accounts payable　应付账款
accounts receivable　应收账款
accrued liabilities　应计负债
cash basis system　收付实现制

check book　支票本
common stock　普通股
cost of goods　产品成本
cost of goods sold　销售成本
credit balance　贷方余额

credit card statement 信用卡对账单	record-keeping system 记账制度
debit balance 借方余额	retained earnings 保留收益
fixed asset 固定资产	single entry accounting 单式记账
notes payable 应付票据	

Para. [2]

1. A debit is that portion of an accounting entry that either increases an asset or expense account, or decreases a liability or equity account.

   这句话中的 either... or... 连接了动词 increase 和 decrease。本句解释了会计分录的借记部分既可以表示增加，也可以表示减少。资产账户和花费账户的增加，以及债务账户和权益账户的减少都属于借记部分。

Paras. [3] to [4]

2. Gain on sale of asset (gain account: normally a credit balance); Loss on sale of asset (loss account: normally a debit balance)

   资产销售盈利的增加是贷记，资产销售亏损是借记。前者通常为贷记余额，后者则是借记余额。

3. You buy $1,000 of goods with the intention of later selling them to a third party.

   本句中的短语 with the intention of doing sth 也可用于 intend to do sth。本句的意思是：你买了 1000 美元的货物，打算日后销售给第三者。

4. The second entry is a $1,000 debit to the cost of goods sold (expense) account and a credit in the same amount to the inventory (asset) account. This records the elimination of the inventory asset as we charge it to expense.

   This records the elimination of the inventory asset 的意思是"把取消存货资产记录了下来"；charge... to... 指"把……记到……的账上"。这句话说明，原来花费 1 000 美元购买的货物已经借记入（资产）存货账户，如今销售出去了，就要将这 1 000 美元借记入已售商品成本（资产费用账户），贷记入资产存货账户。这个分录就等于取消了存货资产，因为这笔账记入了费用账户。

5. When netted together, the cost of goods sold of $1,000 and the revenue of $1,500 result in a profit of $500.

   句中的 When netted together 是省略状语从句，完整的表达应为 When it is netted together，其中的 net 作动词，意思是"总共赚得利润"。名词短语 the cost of goods sold of $1,000 的意思是"出售货物的成本是 1000 美元"。全句的意思是：总的获利情况为，产品本钱 1000 美元，收入 1500 美元，利润 500 美元。

 **Exercises**

Ex. 1 Decide whether the following statements are true (T) or false (F) according to the information in Passage A.

(1) Whether double entry system or single entry system, every transaction is recorded in at least two accounts. (   )

(2) That the transaction is out of balance indicates that something is wrong with it. (   )

(3) A credit indicates the decrease in an asset and expense account and increase in a liability and equity account. (   )

(4) Liability accounts include accounts payable, accrued liabilities, notes payable, common stock, loss on sale of asset, etc. (   )

(5) Inventory and cash are both under the asset account. (   )

(6) A credit to the cash implies the decrease of the cash. (   )

(7) "A debit to the wage (expense) account" means the increase of the expense. (   )

(8) "A credit of $10,000 to the notes payable (liability) account" means the increase of the liability. (   )

(9) "The entry is a total of $6,000 debited to several expense accounts" means the increase of the expense accounts. (   )

(10) Revenues, expenses, gains, and losses are other forms of assets and liabilities. (   )

Ex. 2 Match each of the in the box words to the following phrases or definitions that is most closely related.

A. gain	B. loss	C. entry	D. accrual
E. profit	F. supplier	G. alternative	H. version

(1) relating to or being a method of accounting that recognizes income when earned and expenses when incurred regardless of when cash is received or disbursed

(2) the excess of the selling price of goods over their cost

(3) a person or organization that provides something needed such as a product or service.

(4) (of one or more things) available as another possibility

(5) the profit you receive

(6) a particular form of something differing in certain respects from an earlier form or other forms of the same type of thing

(7) record of a financial transaction in its appropriate book of account

(8) an amount by which the cost of something exceeds its selling price

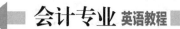

Ex. 3 Use the words mentioned in Ex. 2 to complete the following sentences. Change the form if necessary.

(1) _____ accounting records revenues and expenses when they are incurred, regardless of when cash is exchanged.

(2) Land for farming purposes is expensive, and wages are high, leaving small _____, unless it happens that a man, with his family to assist him, works his own land.

(3) A capital _____ is an increase in the value of an investment.

(4) By changing its _____, the company saved thousands of pounds in import duty.

(5) The distributors will probably bump up the price of the software when the next _____ is released.

(6) A capital _____ is a decrease in the value of an investment.

(7) Drivers are advised to seek _____ routes.

(8) A double _____ accounting system established the accounting equation where assets must always equal liabilities plus owner's equity.

Ex. 4 Fill in the blanks with the words given below. Change the form if necessary.

convert	debit	credit	swap
trigger	charge	consume	match

(1) Large price increases could _____ demands for even larger wage increases.

(2) The purchase _____ to her account.

(3) Every debit that is recorded must be _____ with a credit.

(4) Company XYZ sells $1,000,000 worth of widgets to John Doe for cash. On the balance sheet, the accountants would _____ cash by $1,000,000 (that is, increase cash) and inventory by $1,000,000.

(5) I'd like _____ some RMB to US dollar, please.

(6) Health experts advise that the average woman should _____ about 2,000 calories a day and a man about 2,500 calories to maintain a healthy weight.

(7) We _____ e-mail addresses at the conference, and are planning to work on a couple of projects together.

Ex. 5 Read the following passage and then complete the multiple choices.

What Is a Debit and Credit Balance

Debit balance: In accounting, a debit balance is the ending amount found on the left side of a general ledger account or subsidiary ledger account.

A debit balance is normal and expected for the following accounts:

Asset accounts such as cash, accounts receivable, inventory, prepaid expenses, buildings, equipment, etc. For example, a debit balance in the cash account indicates a positive amount of cash. (Therefore, a credit balance in cash indicates a negative amount likely caused by writing checks for more than the amount of money currently on hand.)

Expense accounts and loss accounts including cost of goods sold, wages expense, rent expense, interest expense, loss on disposal of equipment, loss from lawsuit, etc. (The debit balances in these accounts will be transferred to retained earnings or to the proprietor's capital account at the end of each accounting year.)

Credit balance: In accounting, a credit balance is the ending amount found on the right side of a general ledger account or subsidiary ledger account.

A credit balance is normal and expected for the following general ledger and subsidiary ledger accounts:

Liability accounts. These include accounts payable, notes payable, wages payable, interest payable, income taxes payable, customer deposits, deferred income taxes, and so on. For instance, a credit balance in accounts payable indicates the amount owed to vendors. (Therefore, a debit balance in a liability account indicates that the company has paid more than the amount owed, has made an incorrect entry, etc.) Since liability accounts are permanent accounts, their balances are not closed at the end of the accounting year.

Equity accounts. Four examples of equity accounts are common stock, paid-in capital in excess of par value, retained earnings, and M. Smith, Capital. These are also permanent accounts and their balances are not closed at the end of the accounting year.

Revenue accounts and gain accounts. Examples include sales revenues, service revenues, interest revenues, gain on disposal of equipment, gain from lawsuit, etc. Since these accounts are temporary accounts, their balances will be transferred to retained earnings or to the proprietor's capital account at the end of each accounting year.

(1) Which of the following statements is FALSE?

A. The left side of a general ledger account is debit and the right side is credit.

B. In both asset and expense accounts, debit indicates increase and credit decrease.

C. A debit balance in the cash account indicates a positive amount of cash and a credit balance negative amount, meaning the expenditure is more than the revenue.

D. Expense accounts and loss accounts are under the equity account.

(2) Typically a liability account has a credit balance and once a debit balance arises, it indicates _____. Which of the following four statements is FALSE?

A. the company's liability has increased

B. the company has debtors now

C. the company is a creditor now

D. the company has paid more than the amount owed

(3) The credit of revenue and gain accounts indicates the ________ and the debit of revenue and gain accounts ________.

A. increase increase B. increase decrease

C. decrease decrease D. decrease increase

(4) The structure of expense accounts and loss accounts is similar to that of ________ and revenue accounts and gain accounts similar to that of ________.

A. asset accounts cash accounts

B. liability and equity accounts asset accounts

C. asset accounts liability and equity accounts

D. liability and equity accounts liability and equity accounts

(5) The common point of expense accounts and loss accounts, and revenue accounts and gain accounts is that ________. Which of the following four is statements FALSE?

A. both of them are temporary accounts

B. both of them will be transferred to retained earnings or to the equity's accounts

C. the meanings of the credit and debit of both of the accounts are the same

D. the meanings of the credit and debit of both of the accounts are contrary

Passage B

Debits and Credits

[1] Let's take a look at the accounting equation to illustrate the double entry system. Here is the equation with examples of how debits and credit affect all of the accounts.

Accounting Equation							
Assets		=	Liabilities		+	Equity	
Debits ↑ Increase	Credits ↓ Decrease		Debits ↓ Decrease	Credits ↑ Increase		Debits ↓ Decrease	Credits ↑ Increase

Figure 1

[2] As you can see from Figure 1, assets always have to equal liabilities plus equity. In other words, overall debits must always equal overall credits. For example, if an asset account is increased or debited, either a liability or equity account must be increased or credited for the same amount.

[3] This is always the case except for when only affects one side of the accounting equation. For example, if a restaurant purchases a new delivery vehicle for cash, the cash account is decreased by the cash disbursement and increased by the receipt of the new vehicle. This transaction does not affect the liability or equity accounts, but it does affect two different assets accounts. Thus, assets are decreased and immediately increased resulting in a net effect of zero.

Introduction to debits and credits

[4] The initial challenge with double-entry is to know which account should be debited and which account should be credited.

[5] Before we explain and illustrate the debits and credits in accounting and bookkeeping, we will discuss the accounts in which the debits and credits will be entered or posted.

[6] Generally these types of accounts are increased with a debit:

Dividends (Draws);

Expenses;

Assets;

Losses.

You might think of D-E-A-L when recalling the accounts that are increased with a debit.

[7] Generally the following types of accounts are increased with a credit:

Gains;

Income;

Revenues;

Liabilities;

Stockholders' (Owner's) equity.

You might think of G-I-R-L-S when recalling the accounts that are increased with a credit.

[8] To decrease an account you do the opposite of what was done to increase the account. For example, an asset account is increased with a debit. Therefore it is decreased with a credit.

T-accounts

[9] Accountants and bookkeepers often use T-accounts as a visual aid for seeing the effect of the debit and credit on the two (or more) accounts. We will begin with two T-accounts: Cash and Notes Payable.

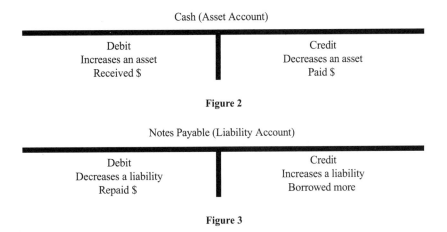

Figure 2

Figure 3

Normal balances

[10] When looking at a T-account for each of the account classifications in the general ledger, here is the debit or credit balance you would normally find in the account:

Table 1

Account Classification	Normal Balance
Assets	Debit
Contra asset	Credit
Liability	Credit
Contra liability	Debit
Owner's equity	Credit
Stockholder's equity	Credit
Owner's drawing or dividends account	Debit
Revenues (or Income)	Credit
Expenses	Debit
Gains	Credit
Losses	Debit

Revenues and gains are usually credited

[11] Revenues and gains are recorded in accounts such as sales, service revenues, interest revenues (or interest income), and gain on sale of assets. These accounts normally have credit balances that are increased with a credit entry.

[12] The exceptions to this rule are the accounts sales returns, sales allowances, and sales Discounts—these accounts have debit balances because they are reductions to sales. Accounts with balances that are the opposite of the normal balance are called contra accounts; hence contra revenue accounts will have debit balances.

[13] Let's illustrate revenue accounts by assuming your company performed a service and was immediately paid the full amount of $50 for the service. The debits and credits are presented in the following general journal format:

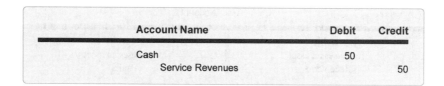

Account Name	Debit	Credit
Cash	50	
Service Revenues		50

Figure 4

[14] Whenever cash is received, the asset account cash is debited and another account will need to be credited. Since the service was performed at the same time as the cash was received, the revenue account service revenues is credited, thus increasing its account balance.

[15] Let's illustrate how revenues are recorded when a company performs a service on credit (i.e., the company allows the client to pay for the service at a later date, such as 30 days from the

date of the invoice). At the time the service is performed the revenues are considered to have been earned and they are recorded in the revenue account service revenues with a credit. The other account involved, however, cannot be the asset cash since cash was not received. The account to be debited is the asset account accounts receivable. Assuming the amount of the service performed is $400, the entry in general journal form is:

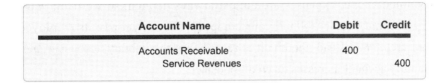

Account Name	Debit	Credit
Accounts Receivable	400	
Service Revenues		400

Figure 5

[16] Accounts receivable is an asset account and is increased with a debit; service revenues is increased with a credit.

Expenses and losses are usually debited

[17] Expenses normally have their account balances on the debit side (left side). A debit increases the balance in an expense account; a credit decreases the balance. Since expenses are usually increasing, think "debit" when expenses are incurred. (We credit expenses only to reduce them, adjust them, or to close the expense accounts.) Examples of expense accounts include salaries expense, wages expense, rent expense, supplies expense, and interest expense.

[18] To illustrate an expense let's assume that on June 1 your company paid $800 to the landlord for the June rent. The debits and credits are shown in the following journal entry:

Account Name	Debit	Credit
Rent Expense	800	
Cash		800

Figure 6

[19] Since cash was paid out, the asset account cash is credited and another account needs to be debited. Because the rent payment will be used up in the current period (the month of June) it is considered to be an expense, and rent expense is debited. If the payment was made on June 1 for a future month (for example, July) the debit would go to the asset account prepaid rent.

[20] As a second example of an expense, let's assume that your hourly paid employees work the last week in the year but will not be paid until the first week of the next year. At the end of the year, the company makes an entry to record the amount the employees earned but have not been paid. Assuming the employees earned $1,900 during the last week of the year, the entry in general journal form is:

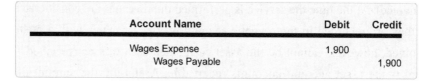

Account Name	Debit	Credit
Wages Expense	1,900	
Wages Payable		1,900

Figure 7

[21] As noted above, expenses are almost always debited, so we debit wages expense, increasing its account balance. Since your company did not yet pay its employees, the cash account is not credited, instead, the credit is recorded in the liability account wages payable. A credit to a liability account increases its credit balance.

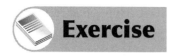 **Exercise**

Decide whether the following statements are true (T) or false (F) according to the information in Passage B.

(1) Credit is contrary to debit, indicating increase in liability and equity accounts and decrease in asset account. (   )

(2) A business transaction is sure to affect two sides of the accounting equation. (   )

(3) "Resulting in a net effect of zero" means the balance of the asset account is not affected. (   )

(4) The problem which account should be debited and which account should be credited is not difficult. (   )

(5) Debit entries are depicted to the left of the T-account and credits are shown to the right of the "T" account. (   )

(6) Figure 3 tells us debit of notes payable account means borrowing more. (   )

(7) That revenues and gains are usually credited means they are increased with a credit entry like equity accounts. (   )

(8) That expenses and losses are usually debited implies that they are under asset accounts. (   )

(9) It's impossible that we credit expenses. (   )

Unit 7

Passage A

Journal Entry

Overview

[1] A journal entry is used to record a business transaction in the accounting records of a business. A journal entry can be recorded in the general ledger, but sometimes in a subsidiary ledger that is then summarized and rolled forward into the general ledger. The general ledger is then used to create financial statements for the business.

[2] The logic behind a journal entry is to record every business transaction in at least two places (known as double entry accounting). For example, when you generate a sale for cash, this increases both the revenue account and the cash account. Or, if you buy goods on account, this increases both the accounts, payable account and the inventory account.

How to write a journal entry

[3] The structure of a journal entry is:
- A header line may include a journal entry number and entry date.
- The first column includes the account number and account name into which the entry is recorded. This field is indented if it is for the account being credited.
- The second column contains the debit amount to be entered.
- The third column contains the credit amount to be entered.
- A footer line may also include a brief description of the reason for the entry.

Thus, the basic journal entry format is:

Table 1

	Debit	Credit
Account name/number	$ xx,xxx	
Account name/number		$ xx,xxx

[4] The structural rules of a journal entry are that there must be a minimum of two line items in the journal entry, and that the total amount you enter in the debit column equals the total amount entered in the credit column.

[5] A journal entry is usually printed and stored in a binder of accounting transactions, with backup materials attached that justify the entry. This information may be accessed by the external auditors as part of their year-end investigation of a company's financial statements and related systems.

Types of journal entries

[6] There are several types of journal entries, including:

- *Adjusting entry.* An adjusting entry is used at month-end to alter the financial statements to bring them into compliance with the relevant accounting framework, such as Generally Accepted Accounting Principles or International Financial Reporting Standards. For example, you could accrue unpaid wages at month-end if the company is on the accrual basis of accounting.

- *Compound entry.* A compound journal entry is one that includes more than two lines of entries. It is frequently used to record complex transactions, or several transactions at once. For example, the journal entry to record a payroll usually contains many lines, since it involves the recordation of numerous tax liabilities and payroll deductions.

- *Reversing entry.* This is typically an adjusting entry that is reversed as of the beginning of the following period, usually because an expense was to be accrued in the preceding period, and is no longer needed. Thus, a wage accrual in the preceding period is reversed in the next period, to be replaced by an actual payroll expenditure.

[7] In general, do not use journal entries to record common transactions, such as customer billings or supplier invoices. These transactions are handled through specialized software modules that present a standard on-line form to be filled out. Once you have filled out the form, the software automatically creates the accounting record for you. Thus, journal entries are not to be used to record high-volume activities.

[8] Journal entries and attached documentation should be retained for a number of years, at least until there is no longer a need to have the financial statements of a business audited. The minimum duration period for journal entries should be included in the corporate archiving policy.

Example

[9] Analyzing transactions and recording them as journal entries is the first step in the accounting cycle. It begins at the start of an accounting period and continues during the whole

period. Transaction analysis is a process which determines whether a particular business event has an economic effect on the assets, liabilities or equity of the business. It also involves ascertaining the magnitude of the transaction i.e., its currency value.

[10] After analyzing transactions, accountants classify and record the events having economic effect via journal entries according to debit-credit rules. Frequent journal entries are usually recorded in specialized journals, for example, sales journal and purchases journal. The rest are recorded in a general journal.

[11] The following example illustrates how to record journal entries:

[12] Company A was incorporated on January 1, 2018 with an initial capital of 5,000 shares of common stock having $20 par value. During the first month of its operations, the company engaged in following transactions:

Table 2

Date	Transaction
Jan. 1	An initial capital of 5,000 shares of common stock having $20 par value, $100,000.
Jan. 2	An amount of $36,000 was paid as advance rent for three months.
Jan. 3	Paid $60,000 cash on the purchase of equipment costing $80,000. The remaining amount was recognized as a one year note payable with interest rate of 9%.
Jan. 4	Purchased office supplies costing $17,600 on account.
Jan. 13	Provided services to its customers and received $28,500 in cash.
Jan. 13	Paid $17,600 the accounts payable on the office supplies purchased on Jan. 4.
Jan. 14	Paid wages to its employees for first two weeks of Jan., aggregating $19,100.
Jan. 18	Provided $54,100 worth of services to its customers. They paid $32,900 and promised to pay the remaining amount.
Jan. 23	Received $15,300 from customers for the services provided on Jan. 18.
Jan. 25	Received $4,000 as an advance payment from customers.
Jan. 26	Purchased office supplies costing $5,200 on account.
Jan. 28	Paid wages to its employees for the third and fourth week of January: $19,100.
Jan. 31	Paid $5,000 as dividends.
Jan. 31	Received electricity bill of $2,470.
Jan. 31	Received telephone bill of $1,494.
Jan. 31	Miscellaneous expenses paid during the month totaled $3,470

[13] Table 3 shows the journal entries for the above events.

Table 3

Date	Account Name	Debit	Credit
Jan. 1	Cash	100,000	
	Common Stock		100,000
Jan. 2	Prepaid Rent	36,000	

(Continued)

Date		Account Name	Debit	Credit
		Cash		36,000
Jan. 3	Equipment		80,000	
		Cash		60,000
		Notes Payable		20,000
Jan. 4	Office Supplies		17,600	
		Accounts Payable		17,600
Jan. 13		Cash	28,500	
		Service Revenue		28,500
Jan. 13	Accounts Payable		17,600	
		Cash		17,600
Jan. 14	Wages Expense		19,100	
		Cash		19,100
Jan. 18	Cash		32,900	
	Accounts Receivable		21,200	
		Service Revenue		54,100
Jan. 23		Cash	15,300	
		Accounts Receivable		15,300
Jan. 25		Cash	4,000	
		Unearned Revenue		4,000
Jan. 26		Office Supplies	5,200	
		Accounts Payable		5,200
Jan. 28	Wages Expense		19,100	
		Cash		19,100
Jan. 31	Dividends		5,000	
		Cash		5,000
Jan. 31	Electricity Expense		2,470	
		Utilities Payable		2,470
Jan. 31		Telephone Expense	1,494	
		Utilities Payable		1,494
Jan. 31	Miscellaneous Expense		3,470	
		Cash		3,470

[14] At the end of the period, all the journals for the period are posted to the ledger accounts.

New Words

access ['ækses] *n.* 接近，入口

advance [əd'vɑːns] *vt.* 预付　*n.* 预付款

aggregate ['æɡriɡeit] *vt.* 总计，合计

alter ['ɔːltə(r)] *vt. & vi.* 改变，更改

archive ['ɑːkaiv] *n.* 档案；档案文件；档案室　*vt. & vi.* 存档

ascertain [ˌæsə'tein] *vt.* 弄清，确定，查明

auditor ['ɔːditə(r)] *n.* 审计员，查账员

binder ['baində(r)] *n.* 装订物；文件夹

compliance [kəm'plaiəns] *n.* 服从

documentation [ˌdɔkjumen'teiʃn] *n.* 票据；证据；记录

expenditure [ik'spenditʃə(r)] *n.* 花费，支出；费用，经费

footer ['futə(r)] *n.* 页脚

header ['hedə(r)] *n.* 标头；标题

incorporate [in'kɔːpəreit] *vt. & vi.* 组成公司，合并

indent [in'dent] *vt.* 缩进（排印、记账等）

journal ['dʒəːnl] *n.* 日记账；日志；日报

justify ['dʒʌstifai] *vt.* 证明……有理

ledger ['ledʒə(r)] *n.* 分类账

magnitude ['mæɡnitjuːd] *n.* 量级，量值，强度

miscellaneous [ˌmisə'leiniəs] *adj.* 各种各样的，五花八门的

module ['mɔdjuːl] *n.* 模块，课程模块

reverse [ri'vəːs] *vt. & vi.* （使）反转，（使）颠倒；撤销

subsidiary [səb'sidiəri] *adj.* 下属的，附属的，次要的　*n.* 子公司

Special Terms

accounting cycle　会计周期

accounting framework　会计框架；核算框架

adjusting entry　调整记录，调整分录

advance rent　预付租金

archiving policy　归档策略

backup materials　备用材料，辅助材料

binder of accounting transactions　会计交易的活页夹

compound journal entry　复合分录

customer billing　客户账单

debit-credit rules　借记贷记规则

footer line　页脚线

general ledger　总账，总分类账

header line　标题行

International Financial Reporting Standards　国际财务报告标准

journal entry　日记账分录，流水分录

on account　赊购，分期付款

reversing entry　冲销或更正分录，转回分录

software modules　软件模块

subsidiary ledger　子分类账，明细分类账

wage accrual　应付工资

Paras. [1] to [2]

1. A journal entry can be recorded in the general ledger, but sometimes in a subsidiary ledger that is then summarized and rolled forward into the general ledger.

    journal entry 为"日记账分录"，general ledger 为"总分类账"。本句的意思是：日记账分录可以直接记入总分类账，有时候也可记入子分类账，这个子分类账归纳后再进入总分类账。

2. Or, if you buy goods on account, this increases both the accounts, payable account and the inventory account.

    本句中的 on credit 意为"赊账"，而 on account 可以指"全部欠款"(= on credit)。

Para. [4]

3. The structural rules of a journal entry are that there must be a minimum of two line items in the journal entry, and that the total amount you enter in the debit column equals the total amount entered in the credit column.

    这句讲解的是日记分录账的结构规则，其后有两个由 that 引导的表语从句。第一个从句意为"至少有两列项目，即贷记和借记"；第二个从句意为"借记栏的总和必须等于贷记栏的总和"。

Paras. [6] to [8]

4. ... to alter the financial statements to bring them into compliance with the relevant accounting framework, such as Generally Accepted Accounting Principles or International Financial Reporting Standards.

    alter the financial statements 指"改变财务报表"，the relevant accounting framework 指"相关的会计框架"。

5. This is typically an adjusting entry that is reversed as of the beginning of the following period, usually because an expense was to be accrued in the preceding period, and is no longer needed.

    本句中的 as of 是一个复合介词，英语释义为 to indicate the time or date from which something starts，即"自……起"；an expense was to be accrued in the preceding period, and is no longer needed 说明在前面的会计期内应计的花费并没有发生，这样上个会计期应计工资就要到下一个会计期转回，使用实际的工资开销替换。

Para. [9]

6. It also involves ascertaining the magnitude of the transaction i.e., its currency value.

本句中的动词 involve 意为"牵涉", 其后接动词的 -ing 形式, 即 ascertaining the magnitude of the transaction, 意为"确定交易的量级", 即"币值"。

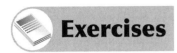 **Exercises**

Ex. 1 Decide whether the following statements are true (T) or false (F) according to the information in Passage A.

(1) Once information has been recorded in a subsidiary ledger, it is periodically summarized and posted to an account in the general ledger. (　　)

(2) Buying goods will increase both the accounts payable account and the inventory account. (　　)

(3) The total amount in the debit column must be equal to that of the credit one. (　　)

(4) Backup materials attached to the journal entry verify the truth of the entry. (　　)

(5) Under the accrual basis of accounting, unpaid wages that have been earned by employees should be entered as wages payable or accrued wages payable. (　　)

(6) Now all the transactions can be handled by online software instead of using journal entries. (　　)

(7) Transaction analysis takes place at the end of the accounting period. (　　)

(8) Sales journal and purchases journal are frequent journal entries. (　　)

(9) 5,000 shares of common stock with $20 par value, the amount value of which is $100,000. (　　)

(10) Advance rent is prepaid rent, which is like the asset and should be debited in the journal entry. (　　)

Ex. 2 Match each of the words in the box to the following phrases or definitions that is most closely related.

A. journal	B. ledger	C. magnitude	D. module
E. subsidiary	F. expenditure	G. framework	H. access

(1) the great size or extent of something

(2) any of a number of distinct but interrelated units from which a program may be built up or into which a complex activity may be analysed

(3) subordinate or secondary

(4) an account book of final entry, in which business transactions are recorded

(5) an amount of money spent

(6) a means of approaching or entering a place

(7) a record of financial transactions in order by date

(8) a basic conceptional structure

Ex. 3 Use the words mentioned in Ex. 2 to complete the following sentences. Change the form if necessary.

(1) Programs are composed of one or more independently developed _____ that are not combined until the program is linked.

(2) Many of the companies in this country consist of _____ which are simply assembly or warehousing operations.

(3) Accounting software has eliminated the need to first record routine transactions into a(n) _____.

(4) The country's debt this year will be of the same order of _____ as it was last year.

(5) Detail-level information for individual transactions is stored in one of several possible journals, while the information in the journals is then summarized and transferred (or posted) to a(n) _____.

(6) Inequalities of income would lead to even greater inequalities in _____ to health care.

(7) We need to establish a legal _____ for the protection of the environment.

(8) Every company must keep control of its income and _____.

Ex. 4 Fill in the blanks with the words given below. Change the form if necessary.

accrue	aggregate	alter	archive
ascertain	incorporate	attach	access

(1) NOAA (National Oceanic and Atmospheric Administration) will analyze _____ data from satellites.

(2) Take time _____ what services your bank is providing, and at what cost.

(3) This company is about _____ with its parent company.

(4) The recording of wages that have been earned but not yet paid or processed through the routine payroll entries is referred to as _____ wages.

(5) Some banks charge if you _____ your account to determine your balance.

(6) Use this cable _____ the printer to the computer.

(7) Unemployment has come down slightly but this does not _____ the fact that it is still a major problem.

(8) They _____ the demands of citizens and communicate these to government officials.

Ex. 5 Fill in the blanks with the words or terms given below.

A. automatically	B. business transactions
C. posted	D. debited/credited
E. general ledger	F. credited/debited
G. journal entry	H. by date

What Is a Journal Entry

In manual accounting or bookkeeping systems, business transactions are first recorded in a journal... hence the term journal entry. A manual (1) _____ that is recorded in a company's general journal will consist of the following: the appropriate date, the amount(s) and account(s) that will be (2) _____, the amount(s) and account(s) that will be (3) _____, a short description/memo, and a reference such as a check number.

These journalized amounts (which will appear in the journal in order (4) _____ are then (5) _____ to the accounts in the (6) _____.

Today, computerized accounting systems will (7) _____ record most of the business transactions into the general ledger accounts immediately after the software prepares the sales invoices, issues checks to creditors, processes receipts from customers, etc. The result is we will not see journal entries for most of the (8) _____.

Passage B

Posting Journal Entries to Ledger Accounts

[1] The second step of accounting cycle is to post the journal entries to the ledger accounts.

[2] The journal entries recorded during the first step provide information about which accounts are to be debited and which to be credited and also the magnitude of the debit or credit (see debit-credit-rules). The debit and credit values of journal entries are transferred to ledger accounts one by one in such a way that debit amount of a journal entry is transferred to the debit side of the relevant ledger account and the credit amount is transferred to the credit side of the relevant ledger account.

[3] After posting all the journal entries, the balance of each account is calculated. The balance of an asset, expense, contra-liability and contra-equity account is calculated by subtracting the sum of its credit side from the sum of its debit side. The balance of a liability, equity and contra-asset account is calculated the opposite way i.e., by subtracting the sum of its debit side from the sum of its credit side.

[4] The ledger accounts shown below are derived from the journal entries of Company A in Passage A.

Table 1

Cash		Accounts Receivable	
$100,000	$36,000	$21,200	$15,300
28,500	60,000		
32,900	17,600		
15,300	19,100		
4,000	19,100		
	5,000		
	3,470		
Balance $20,430		Balance $5,900	

Table 2

Office Supplies	Prepaid Rent	Equipment
$17,600	$36,000	$80,000
5,200		
Balance $22,800	Balance $36,000	Balance $80,000

Table 3

Accounts Payable		Notes Payable	
$17,600	$17,600		$20,000
	5,200		
Balance	$5,200	Balance	$20,000
Utilities Payable		Unearned Revenue	
	$2,470		$4,000
	1,494		
Balance	$3,964	Balance	$4,000

Table 4

Common Stock	
	$100,000
Balance	$100,000

Table 5

Service Revenue		Dividend	
	$28,500	$5,000	
	$54,100		
Balance	$82,600	Balance $5,000	

Table 6

Wages Expense		Miscellaneous Expense	
$19,100		$3,470	
19,100			
Balance $38,200		Balance $3,470	
Electricity Expense		**Telephone Expense**	
$2,470		$1,494	
Balance $2,470		Balance $1,494	

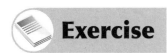 **Exercise**

Decide whether the following statements are true (T) or false (F) according to the information inPassage B.

(1) The first step refers to the journal entries. (   )

(2) "Post" means here "transfer". (   )

(3) The ledger account is composed of asset account and liability and equity accounts. (   )

(4) The relevant ledger account refers to asset account and liability and equity accounts. (   )

(5) The debit amount of a cash journal entry should be transferred to the debit side of the cash ledger account. (   )

(6) The debit side of contra-liability account indicates decrease as that of liability account. (   )

(7) The balance of the cash account is the result of subtracting the sum of the credit side from the sum of its debit side and it is typically a debit balance. (   )

(8) Typically the liability balance is a debit balance, by subtracting the sum of its debit side from the sum of its credit side. (   )

(9) The cash balance $20,430 = the sum of the debit side ($100,000 + $28,500 + $32,900 + $15,300 + $4,000) – the sum of the credit side ($36,000 + $60,000 + $17,600 + $19,100 + $19,100 + $5,000 + $3,470). (   )

(10) Accounts payable are liability accounts, the balance of which is credit. (   )

Unit

8

Passage A

Breakeven Analysis—Fixed Cost, Variable Cost and Profit

Definition

[1] A breakeven analysis is used to determine how much sales volume your business needs to start making a profit, based on your fixed costs, variable costs, and selling price.

[2] The breakeven analysis is often used in conjunction with a sales forecast when developing a pricing strategy, either as part of a marketing plan or a business plan.

How to do a breakeven analysis

[3] To conduct a breakeven analysis, use this formula: Fixed costs divided by (Revenue per unit—Variable costs per unit).

Fixed costs

[4] Fixed costs are costs that must be paid whether or not any units are produced. These costs are "fixed" over a specified period of time or range of production. Examples of fixed costs include:

- Business premises lease (or mortgage) costs over the contract period;
- Startup loan payments (if you financed the business startup costs);
- Property taxes;
- Insurance;
- Vehicle leases (or loan payments if the vehicle is purchased);
- Equipment (machinery, tools, computers, etc.);
- Payroll (if employees are on salary);
- Some utilities—for example, land line phone and internet charges may not change on a month to month basis;
- Accounting fees.

[5] For an existing business fixed costs are readily available. For new businesses make sure to do your research and get the most accurate figures available.

Variable costs

[6] Unit variable costs are costs that vary directly with the number of products produced. For instance, the cost of the materials needed and the labor used to produce units isn't always the same. Examples of variable costs include:

- Wages for commission-based employees (such as salespeople) or contractors;
- Utilities costs that increase with activity—for example, electricity, gas, or water usage;
- Raw materials;
- Shipping costs;
- Advertising (can be fixed or variable);
- Equipment repair;
- Sales costs (such as credit card processing fees, etc.).

Sample breakeven computation

[7] Suppose that your fixed costs for producing 30,000 widgets are $30,000 a year. Your variable costs are $2.20 materials, $4.00 labor, and $0.80 overhead, for a total of $7.00. If you choose a selling price of $12.00 for each widget, then: $30,000 divided by ($12.00–7.00) equals 6,000 units. This is the number of widgets that have to be sold at a selling price of $12.00 to cover your costs. Each unit sold beyond 6,000 generates $5 profit.

Fixed Costs for 30,000 widgets (per year)	
Business lease	$15,000
Property taxes	$5,000
Insurance	$4,000
Equipment	$3,000
Utilities	$3,000
Total fixed Costs	$30,000
Variable Costs (per unit produced)	
Materials	$2.20
Labor	$4.00
Overhead	$0.80
Total variable Cost (Per Unit)	$7.00
Breakeven	
Selling price per unit	$12.00
Selling price—variable costs	$5.00
#Units to sell/year to breakeven ($30,000 / $5.00)	6,000
Profit targets	
#Units to sell/year to generate $10,000 profit	8,000
#Units to sell/year to generate $50,000 profit	**16,000**

Using breakEven calculations

[8] Breakeven analysis allows you to compute various "what if?" scenarios to reduce your breakeven point and increase profits.

- Increasing the selling price—in the above example, if you were able to increase the selling price by $1 you would only need to sell 5,000 units to break even ($30,000 / ($13–$7). Selling 6,000 units would give you a profit of $6,000 (1,000 units multiplied by $6 cost per unit). However, in a highly competitive environment increasing the selling price is often not an option.

- Reducing your fixed costs—if you were able to reduce your fixed costs by $5,000 you would also reduce the breakeven point to 5,000 units sold. Reducing rent and payroll are common ways for businesses to reduce fixed costs, as is relocating to other jurisdictions that have lower business taxes or utilities costs.

- Reducing variable costs—reducing the variable costs by $1 would also lower the breakeven point 5,000 units. Variable costs are typically lowered by reducing material or labour costs, for example, a builder sourcing lumber from a lower-cost supplier or taking advantage of equipment and/or technology to automate production.

- Increasing sales—assuming breakeven unit sales of 6,000, increasing the number of units sold to 10,000 would give a profit of $20,000 (4,000 units multiplied by $5 cost per unit). This calculation can be used when considering the benefits of advertising. Say for example you decide to increase your advertising budget by $5,000 per year, which would raise your fixed costs to $35,000. This would raise your breakeven unit sales to 7,000— anything less means your ad campaign was not successful.

New Words

breakeven ['breik'iːvən] *n.* 盈亏平衡点，收支平衡点

commission-based [kə'miʃn-beist] *adj.* 基于佣金的

campaign [kæm'pein] *n.* 广告宣传；竞选运动

conjunction [kən'dʒʌŋkʃn] *n.* 连接

contractor [kən'træktə(r)] *n.* 承包人，合同工

jurisdiction [ˌdʒuris'dikʃn] *n.* 管辖权，管辖范围；司法权

landline ['lændlain] *n.* 陆地电线；固定电话线路；陆上运输

lease [liːs] *n.* 租金；租约，租契；租赁权 *vt.* 出租，租借

mortgage ['mɔːgidʒ] *n.* 抵押，抵押权；按揭，债权 *vt.* 抵押，按揭

overhead [ˌəuvə'hed] *n.* 管理费用，经常费用

property ['prɔpəti] *n.* 财产，地产；所有权

relocate [ˌriːləu'keit] *vt.& vi.* 迁移；重新安置

scenario [sə'naːriəu] *n.* 方案；剧本

source ['sɔːs] *vt. & vi.* 寻求（尤指供货）的来源

sourcing ['sɔːsiŋ] *n.*采购

variable ['veəriəbl] *adj.* 变化的，可变的

widget ['widʒit] *n.* 小部件，小饰品

Special Terms

accounting fees 会计费用

ad campaign 广告宣传，广告活动

breakeven 收支平衡；保本

breakeven analysis 保本分析，盈亏临界点分析

breakeven computation 保本（点）计算

breakeven point 保本点

business plan 商业计划书

commission-based employee 基于佣金的雇员

contract period 合同有效期

credit card processing fees 信用卡处理费

fixed costs 固定成本

Internet charge 互联网收费

landline phone 固定电话

lease cost 租赁成本

loan payment 偿还贷款

make a profit 盈利

marketing plan 营销计划书，营销报告

pricing strategy 定价策略

processing fee 手续费；处理费；加工费

property tax 不动产税，物业税，财产税

range of production 生产范围

sales cost 销售成本

sales forecast 销售预测

sales volume 销售量，销售额

startup cost 启动成本，创业成本

startup loan 起始贷款，启动贷款

unit variable cost 产品个体变动资本

variable cost 可变成本

Notes

Paras. [1] to [3]

1. A breakeven analysis is used to determine how much sales volume your business needs to start making a profit...

   本句中的 how much 后的从句作动词 determine 的宾语，意为"需要多少销售量才开始盈利"。

2. The breakeven analysis is often used in conjunction with a sales forecast when developing a pricing strategy...

   in conjunction with 指"与……联合 / 配合"，句中意为"保本分析经常与销售预测配合

使用"；when developing a pricing strategy 是一个省略状语从句，省略了主语 + be，结合上下文应该是 your business is，即"当你公司在产生定价策略的时候"。

3. Fixed costs divided by (Revenue per unit–Variable costs per unit).
   固定成本除以产品数量（产品个体收入减去个体可变成本）。

Para. [5]

4. For an existing business fixed costs are readily available. For new businesses make sure to do your research and get the most accurate figures available.
   existing business 指"老企业"；readily available 表示"现成的或确定的"；make sure to do sth. 指"一定要做某件事"。本句的意思是：对于老企业来说，固定成本是确定的。而对新企业一定要进行必要的调查，确认固定成本的准确数额。

Para. [8]

5. ... a builder sourcing lumber from a lower-cost supplier or taking advantage of equipment and/or technology to automate production.
   本句包含两个并列的现在分词短语：sourcing lumber from a lower-cost supplier "从成本低的供应商那里采购木材"和 taking advantage of equipment and/or technology to automate production "利用设备或技术使生产自动化"；短语 take advantage of 等同于 make good use of，指"充分利用"。

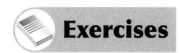 **Exercises**

Ex. 1 **Choose the appropriate answer according to the information in Passage A.**

(1) Which of the following statements is FALSE?

   A. An entity uses breakeven analysis to determine what level of sales are needed to cover total fixed costs.

   B. Total profit at the breakeven point is zero.

   C. In general, a company with lower fixed costs will have a lower breakeven point of sale.

   D. Once you know the fixed and variable costs for the product your business produces you can use that information to calculate your company's breakeven point.

(2) Which of the following statements about the fixed costs and variable costs is FALSE?

   A. Fixed costs are independent of sales volume while variable costs dependent of sales volume.

   B. Fixed costs have nothing to do with the volume of the products.

   C. Variable costs are dependent of the number of products produced.

   D. Variable costs vary with the level of output.

(3) Which one of the following does not belong to fixed costs?

　　A. Property taxes　　　　　　B. Raw materials

　　C. Equipment repair　　　　　D. Wificharges

(4) Which of the following statements about salary and wages is FALSE?

　　A. When an employee is paid on a "salary basis", he or she receives regular pay on a regular basis.

　　B. Someone who is paid wages receives a pay rate per hour, multiplied by the number of hours worked.

　　C. Salary payrolls belong to fixed costs and wages variable costs.

　　D. Payrolls belong to variable costs.

(5) Which one of the following does not belong to variable costs?

　　A. production supplies　　　　B. commissions

　　C. credit card fees　　　　　　D. insurance

(6) Which of the following statements about utilities is TRUE?

　　A. Utilities costs increasing with production are fixed costs.

　　B. It's impossible that utilities do not change during the production.

　　C. Electricity, gas, or water usage charges are fixed costs.

　　D. Landline phone and Internet charges changing month by month belong to fixed costs.

(7) Which of the following options to reduce the breakeven point and increase profits is NOT often adopted?

　　A. Increasing selling price

　　B. Reducing fixed costs

　　C. Reducing variable costs

　　D. Increasing sales

(8) In the sample provided in this passage, if the year profit target is $10,000 it must sell more than _____ units.

　　A. 6,000　　　　B. 8,000　　　　C. 9,000　　　　D. 10,000

Ex. 2 **Match each of the words in the box to the following phrases or definitions that is most closely related.**

A. sourcing	B. payroll	C. overhead	D. mortgage
E. lease	F. contractor	G. commission	H. breakeven

(1) the point in a company or product's development at which revenue equals cost, and neither a profit nor loss is made

(2) a fee paid to an agent or employee for transacting a piece of business or performing a service

(3) a legal agreement by which a bank or other creditor lends money at interest in exchange for taking title of the debtor's property

(4) including all ongoing business expenses not including or related to direct labor or direct

materials used in creating a product or service

(5) the total amount of money that a company pays to its employees

(6) the buying of components of a product from an outside supplier

(7) a contractual arrangement calling for the lessee (user) to pay the lessor (owner) for use of an asset

(8) a person or company that undertakes a contract to provide materials or labor to perform a service or do a job

Ex. 3 **Use the words mentioned in Ex. 2 to complete the following sentences. Change the form if necessary.**

(1) Door-to-door salesmen usually have a low basic wage and earn most of their money on _____ .

(2) Here, as elsewhere, hospital cleaning services were won by a private _____ .

(3) The _____ entitles the holder to use the buildings and any land attached thereto.

(4) The _____ point is the sales volume at which a business earns exactly no money.

(5) A _____ is a company's list of its employees, but the term is commonly used to refer to the total amount of money that a company pays to its employees.

(6) Plan, organize and administrate the _____ and purchasing of supplier.

(7) Many businesses are moving out of New York because the _____ there is so high.

(8) I couldn't make my _____ repayments so the building society repossessed my house.

Ex. 4 **Fill in the blanks with the words given below. Change the form if necessary.**

breakeven	mortgage	lease	source
conduct	make sure	generate	relocate

(1) A good rule of thumb is that a broker must _____ sales of ten times his salary if his employer is to make a profit.

(2) _____ you have a balanced intake of vitamins A, B, C and D.

(3) The company decided _____ to the suburbs because the rent was much cheaper.

(4) The dean asked me _____ experiments with new teaching methods.

(5) She was called upon _____ a supply of carpet.

(6) The Boston Museum of Fine Arts has already contracted _____ part of its collection to a museum in Japan.

(7) He had _____ his house to pay his legal costs.

(8) The company made a small loss last year but this year has managed _____ .

Ex. 5 Fill in the blanks with the words and phrases given below.

A. market control	B. to cover
C. breakeven	D. losses
E. obstacle	F. competitors
G. competitions	H. incurring

Breakeven price is the amount of money for which an asset must be sold to cover the costs of acquiring and owning it. It can also refer to the amount of money for which a product or service must be sold (1) _____ the costs of manufacturing or providing it. In options trading, the break-even price is the stock price at which investors can choose to exercise without (2) _____ a loss.

There are both positive and negative effects from transacting at (3) _____ price. In addition to gaining market shares and driving away existing (4) _____, pricing at breakeven also helps set an entry barrier for new (5) _____ to enter the market. Eventually, this leads to a controlling market position, due to reduced competitions. However, a product or service's comparably low price may create the perception that the product or service may not be as valuable, which could become a(n) (6) _____ to raising prices later on. In the event that others engage in a price war, pricing at breakeven would not be enough to help gain (7) _____. With racing-to-the-bottom pricing, (8) _____ can be incurred when breakeven prices give way to even lower prices.

Passage B

Cost Accounting Basics

[1] Cost accounting basics include capturing costs, organizing these costs and reporting these costs. That's really what it is. However, it can be made complicated with complex products and a large volume of business transactions.

[2] To understand cost accounting basics lets keep it very simple to start. Let's assume you and I own a bird house manufacturing company. We make the very best Tufted Titmouse birdhouses in the world. However, we are just getting our business started and we only have a few costs to start. These costs include:

[3] Building rent $1,000 per month. Heat and electric costs of $300 per month. One birdhouse assembly person we pay $2,000 per month. One truck driver we pay $2,000 per month. Wood to make the birdhouses cost $7 per birdhouse. Office expenses of $500 per month/800 = $.63 per house. We estimate that we can manufacture and sell 40 birdhouses in one day or 800 in a month. So what are our costs to make a birdhouse:

- Building rent = $1,000 per month/800 birdhouses = $1.25 per house;

- Heat and electric= $300 per month/800 houses = $0.38 per house;
- One assembly person = $2,000 per month/800 = $2.50 per house;
- One truck driver = $2,000 per month/800 = $2.50 per house;
- Wood to make one birdhouse = $7.00 per house;
- Office expenses = $500 per month/800 = $0.63 per house.

[4] So, if we add up all our costs for one bird house we come up $14.26 per birdhouse. Excellent, now we know what it costs to make one of our wonderful birdhouses.

[5] Cost accountant types use these cost accounting basics to organize costs into three basic categories:

- Direct material costs;
- Direct labor costs;
- Burden costs.

[6] But, don't let this confuse you. Accountants have an easier way to look at these costs. They think of each of these costs as a bucket. Think of three buckets on the floor. One labeled direct material, one labeled direct labor and one labeled burden. Now let's throw our costs to make a birdhouse into the correct bucket:

- Direct labor is our cost for our assembly person. This person adds value to our birdhouse.
- Direct material is the wood we use to make the birdhouse.
- Burden costs are the other costs

[7] So, after organizing our costs they look like this:

- Direct Labor cost = $2.50 ($2,000 for labor divided by 800 birdhouses);
- Direct Material cost = $7.00;
- Burden costs = $4.75 ($3,800 for burden costs divided by 800 birdhouses).

[8] You may be asking yourself why we bother to put costs into different buckets. The simple answer is so we can analyze these costs and determine better ways to run the business.

[9] For example: Assume that our assembly labor person can make 50% more birdhouses in the same amount of time. Let's see what happens to our costs:

- Direct labor cost is now $1.67 per birdhouse ($2,000 for labor divided by 1,200 birdhouses);
- Direct material remains at $7.00 per birdhouse;
- Burden costs are now $3.17 per birdhouse ($3,800 for burden costs divided by 1,200 birdhouses).

[10] We now make our birdhouses for $11.84 instead of $14.25. I hope you can see the advantage to organizing our costs. Look at how each category of cost acted when we increased our production. If we are able to manufacture another line of birdhouses without increasing our burden costs, then our burden costs per birdhouse would go down for all the birdhouses we manufacture. Since it still costs us $3,800 per month for our burden costs, these costs are then spread out over more birdhouses, therefore, reducing the amount per birdhouse.

[11] Cost accounting basics can be exciting when your analysis and hard work results in

cost improvements for the company. Also, when management knows exactly what the costs are to make their product, it can quote on new work and be certain of the profit it will make. Many companies don't know what their costs are to make a product. The ones that do know their costs have a tremendous advantage.

 **Exercises**

Decide whether the following statements are true (T) or false (F) according to the information in Passage B.

(1) Capturing costs means recognizing all the costs needed to produce products to sell without any missed. (   )

(2) Building rent $1,000 per month is a kind of variable cost. (   )

(3) Heat and electric costs of $300 per month belong to variable cost. (   )

(4) Adding up all the costs for one birdhouse is as follows: $1.25 + $0.38 + $2.50 + $2.50 + $7.00 + $0.63 = $14.26. (   )

(5) Three basic categories of costs have different meanings from three basic types of costs. (   )

(6) Direct labor is the cost for the assembly person and the truck driver. (   )

(7) Assume that our assembly labor person can make 50% more bird houses in the same amount of time, which means the person can make 1,200 bird houses in a month. (   )

(8) The assembly labor person's efficiency affects direct labor cost alone. (   )

(9) The main idea of Para. 11 is the significance of cost accounting basics. (   )

(10) All companies do know what their costs are. (   )

Unit 9

About GAAP

Overview

[1] Financial reporting is the language that communicates information about the financial condition and operational results of a company (public or private), not-for-profit organization, or state or local government.

[2] Specifically, financial reporting includes the following information:

- Financial position (balance sheet, statement of net position);
- Results of operations (statement of revenues, expenses and changes in net position; statement of comprehensive income, etc.), and;
- Disclosures.

[3] The accounting standards developed and established by the Financial Accounting Foundation's (FAF) standard-setting boards—the Financial Accounting Standards Board (FASB) and the Governmental Accounting Standards Board (GASB)—determine how those financial statements are prepared. The standards are known collectively as Generally Accepted Accounting Principles.

[4] For all organizations, GAAP is based on established concepts, objectives, standards and conventions that have evolved over time to guide how financial statements are prepared and presented. For companies or not-for-profits, GAAP is set with the objective of providing information that is useful to investors, lenders, or others that provide or may potentially provide resources.

[5] An additional objective applies to financial reporting for state and local governments: to provide information that enables taxpayers and others who use governmental financial statements to hold governments accountable.

[6] GAAP includes principles on:

- Recognition—What items should be recognized in the financial statements (for example as assets, liabilities, revenues, and expenses);
- Measurement—What amounts should be reported for each of the elements included in financial statements;
- Presentation—What line items, subtotals and totals should be displayed in the financial statements and how might items be aggregated within the financial statements;
- Disclosure—What specific information is the most important to the users of the financial statements. Disclosures both supplement and explain amounts in the statements.

Who sets GAAP?

[7] The Financial Accounting Foundation is the independent, private-sector, not-for-profit organization based in Norwalk, Connecticut responsible for the oversight, administration, financing, and appointment of the Financial Accounting Standards Board and the Governmental Accounting Standards Board. The FASB establishes financial accounting and reporting standards for public and private companies and not-for-profit organizations. The GASB establishes accounting and financial reporting standards for US state and local governments. The FASB and the GASB are responsible for ensuring that GAAP remains the high-quality benchmark of financial reporting so that investors, lenders, capital providers, and other users have access to the information they need to make sound decisions. The FASB is recognized by the Securities and Exchange Commission (SEC) as the designated accounting standard setter for public companies. The FASB's standards are recognized as authoritative by many other organizations, including the State Boards of Accountancy (SBA) and the American Institute of CPAs.

[8] Investors, lenders, and other users of financial information rely on financial reporting based on GAAP to make decisions about how and where to provide financing, and to help financial markets operate as efficiently as possible. The GASB's standards are recognized as authoritative by state and local governments, the State Boards of Accountancy, and the American Institute of CPAs (AICPA). Today, taxpayers, holders of municipal bonds, members of citizen groups, legislators, and oversight bodies rely on this financial information to shape public policy and make investments. These standards also help government officials demonstrate to their stakeholders their accountability and stewardship over public resources. For state and local governments, it is important to note that GAAP is applicable to external financial reporting, and not to budgeting.

The Qualities of GAAP

[9] Companies, not-for-profits, and governments use accounting standards as the foundation upon which to provide users of financial statements with the information they need to provide financing, lend or donate money, or determine how public officials are spending tax dollars.

[10] Investors and citizens trust financial statements that follow GAAP and use this information to assess the financial condition and determine how well an organization or

government manages its resources.

[11] When financial statements are prepared under GAAP, they are based on standards developed by a robust, open due process that results in information that is:

- Relevant, representationally faithful, and reflective of economics;
- Comparable with other organizations or governments;
- Verifiable and auditable by a third party;
- Understood by lenders, investors, donors, taxpayers, and others.

[12] The high-quality financial reporting standards within GAAP are essential to the efficient functioning of our capital markets. For example, GAAP leads to better financial information and is helpful for an organization or government in the following ways:

- To attract the financing they need to hire workers, build plants, and invest in research and development, companies and others organizations must report financial information in a way that investors, lenders, donors, and others find credible and useful.
- Greater comparability in accounting and financial reporting also results in better financing decisions—investors, lenders, and donors make wiser decisions about where to put their money.
- It will also help governments better demonstrate to their citizens and bond holders their stewardship over their government's resources.

[13] High quality financial accounting and reporting standards promote better information in the marketplace. Better information fosters greater transparency. Transparent, relevant information helps investors and lenders make better decisions about where to put their money with confidence. Investors, recognizing the value of high quality financial information, support an objective and inclusive standard-setting process. This "virtuous cycle" ultimately helps make our capital markets more efficient and robust.

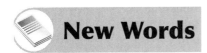

New Words

accountability [ə,kaʊntə'biləti] n. 会计责任

accountable [ə'kaʊntəbl] adj. 有解释义务的

acountancy [ə'kaʊntənsi] n. 会计工作，会计职业；会计学

apply [ə'plai] vt. & vi. 应用；适合

auditable ['ɔ:ditəbl] adj. 可审查的，能审计的

authoritative [ɔ:'θɒrətətiv] adj. 权威的，可信的

benchmark ['bentʃmɑ:k] n. 基准

budget ['bʌdʒit] vt.& vi. 预算　n. 预算

comparability [,kɒmpərə'biləti] n. 可比性

convention [kən'venʃn] n. 公约；惯例；习俗；规矩

credible ['kredəbl] adj. 可信的，可靠的

designate ['dezigneit] *vt.* 指派，选派

disclosure [dis'kləʊʒə(r)] *n.* 披露，公开

donate [dəʊ'neit] *vt. & vi.* 捐赠；献（血）

financing [fai'nænsiŋ] *n.* 筹措资金，理财；融资

foster ['fɒstə(r)] *vt.* 促进

inclusive [in'kluːsiv] *adj.* 包容的，包括的，包罗广泛的

legislator ['ledʒisleitə(r)] *n.* 立法者

municipal [mjuː'nisipl] *adj.* 城市的，市政的

objective [əb'dʒektiv] *n.* 任务，目标 *adj.* 客观的；目标的

oversight ['əʊvəsait] *n.* 监督

representationally [ˌreprizen'teiʃnəli] *adv.* 代表性地

robust [rəʊ'bʌst] *adj.* 强健的，结实的；坚定的

setter ['setə(r)] *n.* 制定者

sound [saʊnd] *adj.* 健全的，完好的

stake [steik] *n.* 股份，重大利益

stakeholder ['steikhəʊldə(r)] *n.* 利益相关者；股东

steward ['stjuːəd] *n.* 管家，干事，理事 *vt. & vi.* 管理，当管事

stewardship ['stjuːədʃip] *n.* 管理工作

subtotal ['sʌbtəʊtl] *n.* 小计

transparency [træns'pærənsi] *n.* 透明，透明度

transparent [træn'speərənt] *adj.* 透明的

virtuous ['vɜːtʃʊəs] *adj.* 有道德的，有德行的；善良的

Special Terms

due process 正当程序

financial position 财务状况

municipal bonds 市政债券，地方政府债券

not-for-profit/nonprofit organization 非营利组织

private-sector 私人部门

standard-setting process 标准制定过程

virtuous cycle 良性循环

Abbreviations

AIA (American Institute of Accountants) 美国会计师协会

AICPA (American Institute of Certified Public Accountants) 美国注册会计师协会

FAF (Financial Accounting Foundation) 财务会计基金会

FASB (Financial Accounting Standards Board) 财务会计标准委员会

GASB (Governmental Accounting Standards Board) 政府会计标准委员会

SBA (State Boards of Accountancy) 国家 / 州会计委员会

SEC (Securities and Exchange Commission) 证券交易委员会

 **Notes**

Paras. [3] to [6]

1. The accounting standards developed and established by the Financial Accounting Foundation's (FAF) standard-setting boards—the Financial Accounting Standards Board (FASB) and the Governmental Accounting Standards Board (GASB)—determine how those financial statements are prepared.

   本句的主语是 The accounting standards，其后有两个修饰语 developed 和 established。本句的谓语为 determine，主语和谓语被主语后置修饰语分割了，这种现象叫作"主谓分隔"。本句的意思是：会计标准是由财务会计基金会的两个标准制定委员会开发和建立的，它们是财务会计准则委员会和政府会计准则委员会。会计标准决定了准备财务报表方法。

2. GAAP is set with the objective of providing information that is useful to investors, lenders, or others that provide or may potentially provide resources.

   动词 set 表示"设置"，be set with the objective 指"设置一个这样的目标"。句中的 that 定语从句中又包含了一个 that 从句。全句的意思是：普遍接受的会计原则设计的目标是完成向投资者、债权人和其他提供资源和潜在提供资源的人提供有用信息的任务。

3. GAAP（普遍接受的会计原则）包括四大原则：权责确认（recognition）原则；数据报告（measurement）原则；呈现（presentation）原则和公开（disclosure）原则。

4. Disclosures both supplement and explain amounts in the statements.

   这句话的主语是 disclosures，由 both... and... 连接了两个谓语动词：supplement 和 explain。本句的意思是：公开原则可以增补和解释报表中的各项数据。

Para. [7]

5. The FASB is recognized by the Securities and Exchange Commission (SEC) as the designated accounting standard setter for public companies.

   短语 recognize... as... 意为"承认……是"。本句的意思是：证券交易委员会承认财务会计准则委员会是它指派的公共公司会计标准的设计者。

Paras. [11] to [13]

6. When financial statements are prepared under GAAP, they are based on standards developed by a robust, open due process that results in information...

   短语 due process 本指法律上的正当程序，应用到会计学上，放在 standards developed

by a robust, open due process 中的意思是"通过健全公开的正当程序所建立起来的会计准则"。

7. Relevant, representationally faithful, and reflective of economics

本句中三个形容词 relevant "中肯的"、representationally faithful "忠实呈现的"和 reflective of economics "真实反映经济状况的"描述了在公认会计准则指导下完成的财务报表所提供的信息质量。

8. To attract the financing they need to hire workers, build plants, and invest in research and development, companies and others organizations must report financial information in a way that investors, lenders, donors, and others find credible and useful.

本句的主语是 companies and others organizations。全句的意思是：为了吸引融资，他们需要雇工，建厂，投资研发。报告财务信息时必须让投资人、债权人、捐献者和其他人员发现所提供的信息可信有用。

9. Investors, recognizing the value of high quality financial information, support an objective and inclusive standard-setting process.

本句主语 investors 和谓语动词 support 被 recognizing the value of high quality financial information 分隔开了。全句的意思是：投资人认识到了高质量的财务信息的价值，他们会支持客观的、具有包容性的标准设计程序。

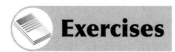

Exercises

Ex. 1 **Decide whether the following statements are true (T) or false (F) according to the information in Passage A.**

(1) "Not-for-profit organization" means that a profit organization is an exception that it is not essential for it to report its financial condition. (   )

(2) Disclosure means making the financial reporting known to all its employees of an enterprise. (   )

(3) The objective of the financial reporting for state and local governments is the same as that of any company or non-profits. (   )

(4) The financial statements have to include the balance sheet according to the GAAP. (   )

(5) According to the principle on disclosure, the amounts in the financial statements are not allowed to be altered. (   )

(6) The FASB and GASB are supervised, administrated, financed and appointed by FAF. (   )

(7) The FASB's standards are so authoritative that they are generally accepted. (   )

(8) Only companies or corporations have their stakeholders, while state and local governments do not. (   )

(9) Investors and citizens trust financial statements, because they believe in the companies and the governments. (   )

(10) The foundation of this "virtuous cycle" is capital markets. (　　)

Ex. 2 Match each of the words in the box to the following phrases or definitions that is most closely related.

A. auditable	B. objective	C. robust	D. credible
E. transparent	F. stake	G. authoritative	H. verifiable

(1) a monetary or commercial interest, investment, share, or involvement in something, as in hope of gain

(2) someone or something having power, influence or the right to control and make decisions

(3) easy to perceive or detect

(4) able to be audited

(5) able to be checked or demonstrated to be true, accurate, or justified

(6) able to be believed; convincing

(7) strong and healthy; vigorous

(8) a specific result that a person or an organization aims to achieve within a time frame and with available resources

Ex. 3 Use the words mentioned in Ex. 2 to complete the following sentences. Change the form if necessary.

(1) New opportunities are opening up for investors who want a more direct _____ in overseas companies.

(2) The company has to make its accounts and operations as _____ as possible.

(3) Companies are required to produce _____ financial statements.

(4) Its consensus rulings have received widespread acceptance, establishing the body as an _____ source of interpretation.

(5) We supported the demands for a thorough and _____ investigation by independent and impartial experts.

(6) If objectives are to be meaningful to people, they must be clear, attainable, actionable, and _____.

(7) The economy is _____ and the stock market has reached unprecedented heights in recent weeks.

(8) The _____ of the research is to gain a better insight into labour market processes.

Ex. 4 Fill in the blanks with the words given below. Change the form if necessary.

evolve	designate	donate	finance
foster	apply	demonstrate	budget

(1) Employees must _____ competence in certain skills before they can work independently.

(2) The new bridge will _____ by the state government.

(3) Its cash crisis has been _____ by declining property values.

(4) Sometimes a new technology doesn't drive the old one out, but only parts of it while forcing the rest _____.

(5) Her goal is to find a company willing _____ money for research.

(6) If you _____ for a particular purpose or period of time, you allocate, save, or set aside certain amounts of money for that purpose or period.

(7) They _____ Mr. Yang as director of the laboratory.

(8) Find out ahead of time what regulations _____ to your situation.

Ex. 5 Translate the short passage below into Chinese with the help of Chinese clues.

Statement of Net Position

The statement of net position reports the following elements of financial statements: assets, deferred outflows of resources, liabilities, deferred inflows of resources, net position.

On a statement of financial position, present both of the following: Deferred outflows of resources in a separate section following assets; deferred inflows of resources in a separate section following liabilities; Present the statement of net position in the format: assets + deferred outflows of resources – liabilities – deferred inflows of resources = net position.

A deferred outflow of resources is a consumption of net assets that is applicable to a future reporting period. Deferred outflows of resources have a positive effect on net position and are reported following assets but before liabilities. A deferred inflow of resources is an acquisition of net assets that is applicable to a future reporting period. Deferred inflow of resources have a negative effect on net position and are reported following liabilities but before equity.

提示：

net position 净资产或净权益；

deferred inflows of resources 递延资源流入，预先收取货币资金而在其后的会计期间确认收入项目，递延资源流入属于负债；

deferred outflows of resources 递延资源流出，预先支付货币资金而在其后会计期间确认费用的项目，递延资源流出属于资产。

Passage B

The Ten Generally Accepted Accounting Principles

[1] The origins of Generally Accepted Accounting Principles (GAAP) go all the way back to 1929 and the stock market crash that caused the Great Depression. Faith in the economy was at an all time low and the government of that time decided that something had to be done to rebuild that faith. Thus, the Securities and Exchange Commission (SEC) was formed with a mission to regulate financial practices. The SEC in turn asked the American Institute of Accountants (AIA) for help in order to examine financial statements and 1936 the concept of GAAP was spoken about for the first time.

[2] The evolution of these accounting standards has taken more than half-a-century and changes are being made even today. Along the way the governing boards have changed as well and in the current era, it is the Financial Accounts Standards Board or FASB that decide the rules of accounting. But the SEC still continues to have enforcement powers.

[3] There are ten basic principles that make up these standards:

(1) The Business as a Single Entity Concept: A business is a separate entity in the eyes of the law. All its activities are treated separately from that of its owners. In legal terms a business can exist long after the existence of its promoters or owners.

[4] (2) The Specific Currency Principle: A currency is specified or reporting the financial statements. In the United States all the numbers have to be expressed in US dollars. Companies who conduct parts of their businesses in foreign currencies have to convert the amounts in US dollars using the prevalent exchange rate while reporting their financial statements.

[5] (3) The Specific Time Period Principle: Financial statements always pertain to a specific time. Income statements have a start date and an end date. Balance sheets are reported on a certain date. This way the readers know during which period the business transactions were conducted in.

[6] (4) The Historical Cost Principle: Historical costs are used for valuing items. The prices at which items were bought and sold are used for the valuations. Real values do change during the course of time due to inflation and recession, but these are not considered for reporting purposes.

[7] (5) The Full Disclosure Principle: The full disclosure principle is always in keen focus what with all the accounting scandals in the news nowadays. It is required that companies reveal every aspect of the functioning in their financial statements.

[8] (6) The Recognition Principle: There is also the recognition principle which states that companies reveal their income and expenses in the same time period in which they were accrued.

[9] (7) The Non-Death Principle of Businesses: The accounting principles assume that businesses will continue to function eternally and have no end date as such.

[10] (8) The Matching Principle: The matching principle states that the accrual system of accounting be used and for every debit there should be a credit and vice versa.

[11] (9) The Principle of Materiality: Then there are a couple of principles which require the bookkeepers to use their judgment. There are inaccuracies in all accounting records. After all, nobody is perfect. But when errors are made how important are they for the book keeper to break his head over. A ten dollar error can be ignored, but not a thousand dollars one. This is where the principle of materiality comes in and this is where the accountants have to use their judgments.

[12] (10) The Principle of Conservative Accounting: Conservative accounting is another principle to be adopted for the good of the company. When expenses happen they are to be recorded immediately, but incomes are to be recorded only when the actual cash has been received. Of course, what policies companies follow depend on their own internal strategy.

[13] Companies need to know the GAAP rules thoroughly. In these times when the banking sector and indeed the whole financial world is under so much scrutiny regulators are taking compliance issues, accounting principles and business practices very seriously. That is why it is essential that every individual in the organization adhere to these rules and principles. Having an effective Finance and Accounting team is critical to ensure the accuracy of financial statements.

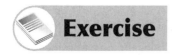 **Exercise**

Decide whether the following statements are true (T) or false (F) according to the information in Passage B.

(1) The Great Depression took place in 1929, when the concept of GAAP was put forward.

(2) The SEC asked the American Institute of Accountants to help to examine financial statements, which led to the discussion of GAAP in 1936.

(3) In the current era the American Institute of Accountants (AIA) decides the rules of accounting.

(4) The life of an entity cannot be longer than its creator.

(5) It is illegal for American companies to conduct their businesses in foreign currencies.

(6) In "financial statements always pertain to a specific time", we can use "apply to" instead of "pertain to".

(7) Inflation and recession lead to price decrease of items.

(8) The revenue recognition principle point out that we recognize the revenue when its generation process has been substantially completed, and an exchange has taken place.

(9) Determining what is a material or significant amount can require professional judgment.

(10) A thousand dollars' error is material for a small or even a large corporation.

Unit 10

Passage A

China's Accounting Standards: Chinese GAAP vs. US GAAP and IFRS

[1] According to PRC Company Law and other relevant regulations, it is compulsory for all types of Foreign Invested Enterprises (FIEs) in China to comply with statutory annual audit and other compliance processes.

[2] The completion of annual statutory audits and settlement of all relevant tax liabilities are prerequisites for FIEs to distribute and repatriate their profits or dividends back to their home country. Failure to do so may result in extra expenses, penalties, or even revocation of their business license.

[3] When preparing annual financial reports, all FIEs are required to follow the Chinese Generally Accepted Accounting Principles (GAAP), also known as *Chinese Accounting Standards* (CAS). The CAS framework is based on two standards:
- *Accounting Standards for Business Enterprises* (ASBEs), and;
- *Accounting Standards for Small Business Enterprises* (ASSBEs).

[4] The Ministry of Finance (MOF) released ASBEs in 2006 and brought them into effect in January 2007. It is widely viewed by the international community that ASBEs are now substantially converged with IFRS, with only some minor discrepancies in wording.

Related: Tax, accounting and audit in China 2017 (9th Edition)

[5] Most FIEs established in China generally adopt ASBEs for their annual financial reports, the structure of which are similar to the Generally Accepted Accounting Principles of the United States and International Financial Reporting Standards (IFRS).

[6] The ASSBEs are the counterpart of IFRS for SMEs, providing unified standards for small-size enterprises. The ASSBEs use the ASBEs as a reference, but are more similar to tax

95

laws in terms of their tax calculation methods, which simplify the process of making adjustments between accounting standards and tax rules. Small-scale enterprises can choose to adopt either the ASBEs or ASSBEs.

[7] Though the CAS are substantially converged with IFRS, there are minor discrepancies between them in some aspects:

- Valuation methods for fixed assets—Under the IFRS, one may choose the valuation method for certain types of fixed assets. The company can value these assets either using the historical cost principle, or by applying a revaluation of assets. CAS, however, only allow fixed assets to be valued according to their historical cost.

- More detailed rules in CAS—For certain items that are common in China, the CAS have more detailed rules than the IFRS. An example would be the merging of two companies controlled by the same entity and having similar interests. CAS require that the comparative figures be restated, whereas there is no specific rule for this in the IFRS.

- More detailed rules in IFRS—Conversely, the IFRS have rules for situations that are uncommon in China, such as more detailed employee benefit plans. Apart from paying employees with company stock, CAS do not address certain types of employee benefits commonly offered by multinationals. Difficulties can arise when the parent company attempts to translate such a package to its Chinese subsidiary. In this case, the company may need to consult with the MOF as to how this transaction should be recorded.

- Delayed implementation of IFRS—When new updates to the IFRS are released, the MOF first reviews them to determine whether the new rules are appropriate for China, and whether it will decide to incorporate them into the CAS. As a result, the adoption of new IFRS standards is often delayed, or does not happen at all. This can lead to further divergence if the countries where other entities of the corporate group are established adopt the new IFRS rules earlier.

Related: Audit and financial services from Dezan Shira & Associates

[8] The problem of different accounting standards is most visible when an overseas parent company requests financial information from its Chinese subsidiary. Converting Chinese financial reports into a target accounting system can be fairly easy for large multinationals, as these companies have sufficient financial support for purchasing specialized software to complete the process.

[9] However, small and medium-sized companies often cannot afford the software needed for such conversions, and instead have to study the divergence of accounting rules and do the conversion manually. As all FIEs are required to prepare financial reports by the end of the fiscal year, it is important for corporate accounting teams to fully understand Chinese accounting practice and ensure correct annual audit processes.

New Words

comply [kəm'plai] *vi.* (with) 遵从

compulsory [kəm'pʌlsəri] *adj.* 强制性的；义务的

converge [kən'və:dʒ] *vt. & vi.* （使）聚集，（使）一致

conversion [kən'və:ʃn] *n.* 变换，转变

counterpart ['kauntəpɑ:t] *n.* 极相似的人或物；配对物

discrepancy [dis'krepənsi] *n.* 不符合（之处）；差异

divergence [dai'və:dʒəns] *n.* 分歧，背离

implementation [ˌimplimen'teiʃn] *n.* 贯彻；成就

merging [mə:dʒiŋ] *n.* 合并

multinational [ˌmʌlti'næʃnəl] *adj.* 多国的；跨国的 *n.* 跨国公司

penalty ['penəlti] *n.* 惩罚；刑罚

prerequisite [ˌpri:'rekwəzit] *n.* 先决条件，前提，必要条件

repatriate [ˌri:'pætrieit] *vt.* 遣返；回国

revaluation [ˌri:vælju'eiʃn] *n.* 再评价，重估计

revocation [ˌrevə'keiʃn] *n.* 废止，撤销

revoke [ri'vəuk] *vt.* 撤销，取消，废除

small-scale ['smɔ:l-'skeil] *adj.* 小规模的，小型的

statutory ['stætʃətri] *adj.* 法定的，法令的；依照法令的

substantially [səb'stænʃəli] *adv.* 本质上，实质上，大体上

wording ['wə:diŋ] *n.* 用词，措辞

Special Terms

business license 营业执照

company law 公司法

comparative figure 比较数字

compliance process 遵守的程序

extra expense 额外费用

fiscal year 财政年度，会计年度

parent company 母公司，总公司

valuation method 估值方法，估价方法，评估方法

 **Abbreviations**

ASBEs (*Accounting Standards for Business Enterprises*)《企业会计准则》

ASSBEs (*Accounting Standards for Small Business Enterprises*)《小企业会计准则》

CAS (*Chinese Accounting Standards*)《中国会计标准》

FIEs (Foreign Invested Enterprises 外国投资企业，外资企业

IFRS (International Financial Reporting Standards) 国际财务报告准则

MOF (Ministry of Finance) 财政部

SMEs (Small and Medium Enterprises) 中小企业

 **Notes**

Paras. [1] to [4]

1. The completion of annual statutory audits and settlement of all relevant tax liabilities are prerequisites for FIEs to distribute and repatriate their profits or dividends back to their home country.

   这句的主语是两个名词短语：The completion of annual statutory audits "完成年度法定审计" 和 settlement of all relevant tax liabilities "缴纳清理相关的税务债务"。

2. It is widely viewed by the international community that ASBEs are now substantially converged with IFRS, with only some minor discrepancies in wording.

   本句中的被动语态 be widely viewed by... 意为 "受到……的广泛关注"；international community 指 "国际社会"；be substantially converged with... 意为 "与……基本一致"。本句的意思是：中国的企业会计准则和国际财务报告准则基本吻合，仅在措辞方面有细微差异。

Paras. [7] to [9]

3. CAS require that the comparative figures be restated, whereas there is no specific rule for this in the IFRS.

   缩略语 CAS 的全称为 Chinese Accounting Standards；副词 whereas 表示对照，相当于 while。

4. Apart from paying employees with company stock, CAS do not address certain types of employee benefits commonly offered by multinationals.

   本句中的 apart from 等于 in addition to。全句的意思是：中国会计标准除了没有发放雇员股份的规定，也没有解决跨国公司通常给予雇员某些类型的福利的问题。

5. This can lead to further divergence if the countries where other entities of the corporate group are established adopt the new IFRS rules earlier.

本句中的 if 从句的主语 the countries 后又有一个定语从句，因此出现了主谓分隔现象。if 从句的主干结构是 the countries adopt the new IFRS rules earlier。全句的意思是：如果公司集团的另外一些实体建立在这些国家，而且很快地采用了国际财务报告的新准则，这就可能导致进一步的分歧。

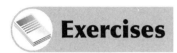 **Exercises**

Ex. 1 **Decide whether the following statements are true (T) or false (F) according to the information in Passage A.**

(1) Annual audit and other compliance processes are essential for all types of FIEs in China. (   )

(2) To distribute and make their profits or dividends go back to their home country, FIEs have to spend extra expense, otherwise, they would be punished or even their business license would be lost. (   )

(3) Chinese Generally Accepted Accounting Principles is also called Chinese Accounting Standards (CAS). (   )

(4) There are differences between IFRS and ASBEs worth paying great attention to. (   )

(5) The structure of the three standards is similar to each other, namely US GAAP, Chinese ASBEs and IFRS. (   )

(6) According to the IFRS, the company can use either historical cost principle or a revaluation to revalue certain types of fixed assets, which accords with the historical cost principle of GAAP. (   )

(7) That CAS does not address certain types of employee benefits commonly offered by multinationals means that CAS doesn't allow multinationals to execute their employee benefit plans. (   )

(8) Without the specialized software the conversion cannot be done manually. (   )

(9) In "the divergence of accounting rules", "divergence" has the same meaning as "difference". (   )

(10) The author of this article holds the view that it's not hard for small and medium-sized companies to do the conversion manually. (   )

Ex. 2 **Match each of the words in the box to the following phrases or definitions that is most closely related.**

| A. compulsory | B. conversion | C. counterpart | D. discrepancy |
| E. multinational | F. penalty | G. revocation | H. wording |

(1) cancellation

(2) a person or thing closely resembling another, especially in function

(3) the act or an instance of converting or the process of being converted

(4) the particular choice of words in which a thing is expressed

(5) required by law or a rule; obligatory

(6) a punishment imposed for breaking a law, rule, or contract

(7) a company operating in several countries

(8) a lack of compatibility or similarity between two or more facts

Ex. 3 **Use the words mentioned in Ex. 2 to complete the following sentences. Change the form if necessary.**

(1) When he was in Europe he went to the bank to handle the _____ of his money into the local currency.

(2) A _____ in the financial reports is the reason for the audit.

(3) Withdrawing the money early will result in a 10% _____.

(4) They tried to prevent the inclusion of any _____ in the statement that would cause offence.

(5) The proposed reforms include making secondary education _____ up to the age of 18.

(6) A number of smaller companies were mopped up by the American _____.

(7) Jeremy was concerned that there would be a _____ of his license after he was pulled over for speeding for the third time this month.

(8) The Foreign Minister held talks with his Chinese _____.

Ex. 4 **Fill in the blanks with the verbs given below. Change the form if necessary.**

comply	converge	merge	revoke
audit	distribute	view	simplify

(1) The World Cup is the most widely-_____ sporting event in the world.

(2) A proposal _____ the two companies was voted through yesterday.

(3) We will introduce legislation _____ trade mark registration and extend the rights they confer.

(4) Do not allow anyone _____ my enterprise server licensor certificate.

(5) Failure _____ with these conditions will result in termination of the contract.

(6) We must try _____ the country's wealth so that we help those who need it most.

(7) Each year they _____ our accounts and certify them as being true and fair.

(8) The systems would only be effective if they were planned to _____ towards an integrated system.

Ex. 5 Translate the short passage below into Chinese.

Dezan Shira & Associates is a pan-Asia, multi-disciplinary professional services firm, providing legal, tax and operational advisory to international corporate investors. Operational throughout China, ASEAN and India, our mission is to guide foreign companies through Asia's complex regulatory environment and assist them with all aspects of establishing, maintaining and growing their business operations in the region. With more than 25 years of on-the-ground experience and a large team of lawyers, tax experts and auditors, in addition to researchers and business analysts, we are your partner for growth in Asia.

Passage B

Differences Between Western and China's Accounting Standards

[1] In Western countries, although amendments and revisions to accounting practices or standards do not have legal binding power, they are formulated according to an existing national legal framework which is provided in most cases by Companies Ordinance or Acts. Companies Ordinance or Acts together with other regulations applicable to individual industries, such as the *Banking Ordinance* for financial institutions and *Listing Rules* or *Securities Acts* for listed or public companies, provide a framework upon which accounting professional bodies formulate accounting and auditing standards. These standards form the basis for establishing accounting principles, and perhaps conventions, that allow enterprises flexibility in formulating their own accounting policies best suited to their individual circumstances. The ultimate objective, in a nutshell, is to produce a set of financial statements that are "true and fair".

[2] Until 1994 China lacked a regulatory framework on which accounting and auditing standards could be set since the country's first national *Companies Laws* were not effective until July 1, 1994. The lack of such a framework also rendered the formulation of other regulations, such as the national *Securities Laws* and *Listing Regulations*, more difficult and time consuming.

[3] Nevertheless, having realized the need for establishing acceptable accounting principles to enable PRC enterprises to attract foreign investment or have their stocks listed on overseas markets, the MOF promulgated a separate set of accounting regulations for selected joint stock companies in January 1992.

[4] In addition, MOF made effective on July 1, 1993, the first set of accounting standards—*Accounting Standards for Enterprises*—applicable to all PRC enterprises. Although it might be confusing at times which accounting regulations or standards would apply, together with the then *Accounting Regulations for Foreign Investment Enterprises of the PRC*, they have provided relatively uniform accounting practices for enterprises to follow in preparing their financial statements. More importantly because of the lack of a complete regulatory and conceptual framework, these accounting rules or regulations are so comprehensive that they encompass

accounting concepts, disclosure requirements, accounting entries, control procedures, record keeping and some aspects of auditing requirements and liquidation.

[5] With the introduction of the *Accounting Law* in 1999, the *Regulations on Financial Reporting of Enterprises* in 2000 and the *Accounting Systems for Business Enterprises* in early 2001, which harmonizes the different accounting standards and regulations applicable to different enterprises, the framework of modern Chinese accounting has finally become clear.

What are the forms and content of financial statements in China?

[6] Under the *Accounting Laws*, the *Regulations on Financial Reporting of Enterprises* and the ASBE, financial statements or reports should comprise a balance sheet, profit and loss accounts, cash flow statements, notes to the accounts and a profit and loss appropriation account. The regulations also cover classification of assets and liabilities in the balance sheet.

[7] The general accounting principles or concepts employed in China's accounting regulations include accuracy, completeness, consistency, comparability, timeliness, materiality, accrual basis, matching, prudence, substance over form and going concern. By and large, the principles mirror those of IAS. Other major features of these regulations are as follows:

- The historical cost convention is prescribed. Assets are required to be recorded at purchase cost (less any necessary impairment provision) and revaluations are strictly prohibited except when allowed by other State provisions.

- The concept of fair market value is not commonly used due to the limited existence of open markets.

- These regulations also require companies to use the calendar year, that is January 1 to December 31, as their financial year.

- The double-entry bookkeeping method should be adopted. Records in accounts and books have to be made in renminbi (yuan) (the lawful currency of the PRC). Transactions and balances denominated in foreign currencies have to be converted into Renminbi at the official rate, which may differ from the current market rate. All records and balances of transactions made in foreign currencies and the exchange rate used must be maintained for reference.

- A clause in these regulations specifically requires the appropriation of a collective Welfare Fund and a Statutory Reserve Fund from profit after tax.

- Due to the infancy of the new systems, certain footnote disclosures may not be as comprehensive as those acceptable elsewhere in the world. Yet, in certain areas, the Chinese standards are extremely stringent. This includes disclosing the corporate identity of related parties and commenting on the fairness of transactions conducted between related parties, and preparing the cash flow statements using both the direct and indirect methods.

[8] The old standards are neither broad nor flexible enough to allow discussion or manoeuvrability on particular subjects. For the first time, ASBE gives management the authority

to exercise professional experience and judgment. While the setting of the ASBE has in theory narrowed the gap between accounting issues in China and those of the Western world, the rigour of applying the ASBE may vary from province to province and from company to company.

What are the auditing requirements in China?

[9] In Western countries limited liability companies are generally subject to an annual audit carried out by independent external auditors whose role is to express an objective opinion on the truthfulness and fairness of the financial statements.

[10] In China, auditing is not a legal requirement but is required under the regulations. Prior to the introduction of the ASBE, the primary objective of auditing in China was to carry out inspection on the financial records of a business to ascertain their accuracy and legality (i.e., whether the transactions conducted complied with relevant State laws and regulations). Auditors in China are concerned with protecting the legal interests of the company as well as the interests of the State. Only with the implementation of the ASBE were the concepts of true and fair presentation introduced.

[11] Prior to 2000 financial statements of state-owned enterprises were not required to be audited annually by independent auditors, but periodical or social audits conducted for the purpose of ascertaining the enterprise's tax liabilities or other purposes might be conducted by the State Audit Bureau or Tax Bureau. Since 2002, except for a few types of specialized industries that have been explicitly exempted, all other State-owned enterprises must be audited at least annually. In addition, the regulations governing the accounting of joint stock companies and foreign investment enterprises require these companies to be subject to annual audit carried out by registered Chinese certified public accounting firms. When reporting on whether the financial statements of foreign investment enterprises are prepared in accordance with the relevant laws and regulations, auditors may make reference to the relevant laws and regulations.

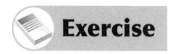 **Exercise**

Decide whether the following statements are true (T) or false (F) according to the information in Passage B.

(1) In Western countries enterprises have flexibility in formulating their own accounting policies best suited to their individual circumstances. (   )

(2) The national *Securities Laws* and *Listing Regulations* of China came into being before 1 July, 1994. (   )

(3) A separate set of accounting regulations for selected joint stock companies were issued by the MOF of PRC in 1994. (   )

(4) Para. 4 implies that in the eyes of the author the problem of a complete regulatory and conceptual framework has been solved. (   )

(5) That these accounting rules or regulations are said to be comprehensive indicates the author was very satisfied with them. (   )

(6) Notes to the accounts provide additional information pertaining to a company's operations and financial position and are considered to be an integral part of the financial statements. (   )

(7) If a company is a going concern, it is planning to liquidate. (   )

(8) The official rate is equal to the current market exchange rate at which one currency may be converted into another. (   )

(9) The State Audit Bureau or Tax Bureau of China is responsible for auditing both state-owned and private enterprises. (   )

(10) Auditors from registered Chinese certified public accounting firms are independent external ones. (   )